DON'T
WAIT

DON'T WAIT

THREE GIRLS WHO WHO FOUGHT FOR CHANGE AND WON

SONALI KOHLI

BEACON PRESS, BOSTON

BEACON PRESS
Boston, Massachusetts
www.beacon.org

Beacon Press books
are published under the auspices of
the Unitarian Universalist Association of Congregations.

27 26 25 24   8 7 6 5 4 3 2 1

This book is printed on acid-free paper that meets the uncoated
paper ANSI/NISO specifications for permanence as revised in 1992.

Text design and composition by Kim Arney

*Library of Congress Cataloguing-in-Publication
Data is available for this title.*
Paperback ISBN: 978-0-8070-1095-2
E-book ISBN: 978-0-8070-1096-9
Audiobook: 978-0-8070-1638-1

*This book is dedicated to
all the brown queer AYAs
who cancer stole.*

*To the ones surviving:
I see you, I am you.
You are enough,
and I am so happy
you're here.*

CONTENTS

Author's Note   ix

PART 1   **THE CATALYST**   1

CHAPTER 1   Nalleli   3

CHAPTER 2   Kahlila   9

CHAPTER 3   Sonia   15

Q&A 1   Critical Self-Reflection   19

                  Discussion Questions   24

PART 2   **KNOW YOUR STORY**   25

CHAPTER 4   Nalleli   27

CHAPTER 5   Kahlila   33

CHAPTER 6   Sonia   39

Q&A 2   Building Your Artistic Toolbox   45

                  Discussion Questions   49

PART 3   **FOOTPRINTS ON THE MOON**   51

CHAPTER 7   Nalleli   53

CHAPTER 8   Kahlila   59

Q&A 3   Find Your Movement   64

                  Discussion Questions   68

CHAPTER 9   Sonia   69

PART 4   **IN THE STREETS (AND BEHIND THE SCREENS)**   **73**

CHAPTER 10   Nalleli   **75**

CHAPTER 11   Kahlila   **79**

CHAPTER 12   Sonia   **87**

Q&A 4   Resolving Conflicts Within
           Movement Work   **92**

           Discussion Questions   **98**

CHAPTER 13   Nalleli   **99**

CHAPTER 14   Kahlila   **105**

CHAPTER 15   Sonia   **109**

CHAPTER 16   Kahlila   **115**

Q&A 5   Caring for Yourself amid
           Movement Work   **119**

           Discussion Questions   **125**

PART 5   **THE FIGHT CONTINUES**   **127**

CHAPTER 17   Nalleli   **129**

CHAPTER 18   Kahlila   **135**

CHAPTER 19   Sonia   **141**

           Discussion Questions   **146**

           Acknowledgments   **147**
           Notes   **151**
           Image Credits for Insert   **159**

AUTHOR'S NOTE

This book addresses a range of difficult experiences that the three primary subjects have confronted and/ or fought against, including domestic abuse, police brutality, mental health challenges, cancer, and reproductive illness. The stories center around each girl's movement work and resilience, and my goal is to always center narratives in realistic hope. Nonetheless, I understand if the topics are difficult and I trust you to care for yourself and know what you are prepared for.

I realize that's a daunting paragraph, but I promise this isn't a book all about struggle and pain. There is some of that. There's also the joy that comes from resistance, from understanding your power and how to wield it for change.

I'm a journalist and for years I wrote about youth activism, but for adult readers. When I'd march the streets alongside teens defending immigration rights or when I'd talk to young people in classrooms, they often wanted to know how to become an activist themselves. What I saw was not the people who are pushed into activism because their life is on the line in a big and obvious and famous way; I saw teenagers who talked to each other and their teachers and tried to understand how to maintain some semblance of control in a world that was constantly changing, where adults gave them so little autonomy but so much responsibility. I saw the conversations, arguments, and challenges of trying to make change while also trying to grow up. The reality is that as teenagers you are powerful; you're also not saviors and shouldn't be tasked with the burden of saving the world.

You're about to read the stories of three activists. You might be surprised as the book jumps between them without a clear connection between their stories. I welcome you to sit with them. To me, the connections are that these are three girls of color fighting for justice in California, a state that is constantly congratulating itself on its liberalism and treatment of its residents. But all three journeys center around experiences of racism—environmental, carceral, and educational—and the power each girl found to make her community better. And the problems we face here, the people working to solve those problems and the way they better their communities, can impact the conversations and decisions in other places around the country.

Throughout this book, you'll find Q&A sections between some chapters that include questions and answers from folks in movement work. These are moments to pause and reflect on the themes the protagonists are facing, with the hope that they are helpful to your own road to make change in your community. Some are interviews that I, the author, conducted, while others are conversations between the young activists and someone who was formative in their movement work, or whose expertise is one they want more people their age to know about.

I consider this a work of nontraditional journalism. As much as possible, I have tried to verify the portions that I was not present to witness. That's why you'll see news stories or government documents cited, and sometimes I've spoken to a second person about an event or watched videos of it. However, in the absence of a secondary source or if the secondary source would have been a government agency representative or "traditional" authority figure the news media approaches regularly for confirmation, I have told the story from the point of view of the activist who experienced it, as she remembers it. What's irrefutable are the timelines: These girls took action, and after that the people who govern in California changed what they spend money on and the rules that protect the communities the activists fought for. What led to those changes and how each student's actions contributed to those changes are told from the activist's point of view. This is an intentional act of re-centering people as experts of their own lives and experiences. I also played with the meaning of *on the record*. Many people don't know what that means, and in my opinion journalists don't do a good enough job explaining it. "On the record" means that as a journalist, I can write anything you say to me—either by quoting or paraphrasing you—and attribute it to you with your full name. When talking to most adults, we journalists are taught that our subjects are on the record if we make it clear that we are journalists working on a story. The same is true for kids, with the addition of getting a parents' or guardians' permission. Once a source says something on the record, they cannot remove it from the record. That's important for public officials who we need to keep accountable, but the same rules did not apply in this book. If an activist shared something and later decided they were not comfortable with it going in a book forever, they were allowed to tell me, and I would not include it. This does not mean they had veto power, or read the book in full, before it was published. It means they had control over what I had the option to share about them.

I paid two of the activists—Kahlila and Sonia—to conduct and record the Q&A interviews. Those are the only portions of the book any of the subjects had direct control over. For the rest of the book, I conducted interviews and spent time with the subjects so I could write these narratives. No one in the book had control over what I wrote, but they did have control over how much access they wanted to give me to their life, feelings, and thoughts; boundaries that I respected.

If you don't like what you see around you—if you want to understand how the world works and how to make change happen, starting in your own community or close to it—then this is the book for you.

Thanks for reading; let's jump in.

DON'T
WAIT

PART 1

THE CATALYST

I'm no longer accepting the things I cannot change. . . . I'm changing the things I cannot accept.

—ANGELA DAVIS,
activist, organizer, and scholar[1]

CHAPTER 1

NALLELI

The scent of fresh guava is sublime. Its aroma is sweet, but not too sweet—like not juices-drip-down-your-chin sweet, but succulent, a little floral, stronger the longer it sits on your counter. Fresh guava smells like the backyard at Nalleli's big brother's house, like her family's homes in Mexico.

This smell that wafts through her Los Angeles apartment is not fresh guava. It is cloying, fake. Instead of anticipation of a sweet bite, you feel a headache coming on when you smell it. It's like someone tried to make a guava air freshener to hide what their house actually smelled like.

Which is, Nalleli Cobo had just learned, pretty much exactly what was happening across the street. Her neighbor wasn't a house, though; it was an oil field. And now it was a dark weekday night and Nalleli was standing outside the oil field, facing down a giant wall shielding the monstrosity that might be destroying her family from the inside out.

With flip phones lighting the way, Nalleli and her mom made the too-short trek across the street, to the wall that they had until now walked past every day for years without a second thought—Nalleli on her way to school, and her mom on her way to work. They had just left a meeting that had Nalleli feeling like a thousand lightbulbs were suddenly alight in her head. Nalleli, like many children, judged the normalcy of her childhood based on what she saw online and on TV. By that measure, she knew she didn't have a typical childhood because no one on the Disney Channel had to sleep sitting up so they wouldn't choke on their nosebleeds. Those kids talked about who scored what at the soccer game. Nalleli and her friends talked about who was feeling sick that day and whether the air smelled like fake chocolate or fake guayaba.

She had never had an answer for why, until now. That evening, Nalleli and her mom gathered in the community room of an apartment building down the street from theirs in South Central Los Angeles, close to the University of Southern California campus. A group of doctors who study toxins had come to talk to residents about the oil well across the street. All Nalleli had known about it was that sometimes she saw a tall yellow structure rise up and down over the high walls. She had thought it was a roller coaster. She couldn't wait to visit the amusement park someday.

Nalleli, the youngest in the room, listened as these adults rattled off the pollution and chemicals that the oil company released in trying to collect their liquid gold and the symptoms you could experience if those poisons seeped into your body. She didn't understand or remember the long chemical names, but she did recognize their effects.

Nausea? Check.

Nosebleeds? Check.

Headaches? Check.

Heart palpitations? Check.

Every day, people use oil. They drive cars, they fly planes, and huge companies make all the stuff that people want to buy and wear and throw away. But they're not thinking about, or at least don't seem to care enough about, what harvesting that oil does to kids like Nalleli, whose body would regularly freeze up without warning.

Nalleli hadn't thought about any of that either, until those doctors told her there was poison across the street. She felt betrayed. So did her mom. They had to learn more. They had already suffered so much—there was no more time to lose. That's why they snuck across the street and tried to read the signs that night, as soon as the meeting ended. There were so many signs on this wall that they'd never bothered to read before. But the phone lights weren't bright enough, ten-year-old Nalleli wasn't tall enough, and her mom was not confident enough in her English-reading skills to make out the warnings. They would have to wait until morning to figure out what was on the other side of the wall.

The next morning, refreshed by sleep and aided by sunlight, Nalleli and her mom left home ten minutes early to investigate. Once there, Nalleli read aloud the signs, from top to bottom, some posted taller than she was. Beside the large white gates that were always closed was a sign in the shape of a diamond made of different-colored panels that Nalleli had thought was pretty. Now her mother explained the colors, along with their corresponding numbers, warned of the dangers behind the wall—red, or 4, for fire hazard; blue, or 3, for health hazard and yellow, or 2, for unstable materials. This site had 3s and 4s—the most dangerous levels.

There was another sign, too, that still lives in Nalleli's mind. It warned that the site may contain toxic chemicals known to the state of California to cause reproductive harm, birth defects, and cancer.

For most people outside the city, Los Angeles is the land of Hollywood and glamour. But for Nalleli, from this day forward, she saw a different reality—one of the biggest urban oil fields in the country.

Now she couldn't sit through a drive without noticing wells that were hidden in plain sight all over the city. That fancy office building in Beverly Hills? Actually just beautified walls meant to hide an oil well. The synagogue in Pico Robertson? It looks like a house of worship in the largely Jewish neighborhood, but there's just machinery pumping within.[1] The machines digging into the ground at the Baldwin Hills park where Nalleli played? Oil wells. She hadn't noticed them before, and as Nalleli and her mom began to research why they lived so close to one, they found they were far from alone. But even though there were more than a thousand oil wells that were either being used or ready to be used in Los Angeles, she knew not all of them impacted the local communities the way hers did.[2]

At a doctor's appointment not long after that meeting, in search of a way to fix Nalleli's heart palpitations, her mom mentioned the oil well across the street to the doctor. He raised his glasses to the top of his head, looked at her dead in the eye, and said, "You have to move."

"If I do move, another family is just going to take my place," she said. On top of the money they'd need to move, it felt wrong to leave someone else with a home that could poison them.

The answer, then, was to fight. And they did, for the rest of Nalleli's teen years.

If the next decade of Nalleli's life was a movie montage, here's what you'd see:

Nalleli and her mom knocking on neighbors' doors when they smelled the chemicals from the well so that people from at least nine different homes would call authorities and air quality control officials would be forced to send someone out to investigate.

Preteen Nalleli in her green Catholic school uniform, telling off the Los Angeles City Council for not taking better care of her community. Then, taking a picture in the very center of the dais, pronouncing that she could see herself there.

Being interviewed for *Los Angeles Times* stories about the campaign she and her mom started—People Not Pozos (oil wells in Spanish)—to make sure oil wells are located farther from homes.[3] Standing next to a United States senator who read the story and lent her support. Watching as the oil well was finally shut down.

A marching teenage Nalleli at the Los Angeles climate strike alongside Swedish climate activist Greta

Thunberg, looking out onto a mass of people who held up posters with her face on it.

Nalleli graduating high school and starting college nearby, with plans to become a civil rights lawyer.

And throughout it all: pain. So much pain that she would sometimes pass out. Five years of doctors' appointments without any answers or relief. And then, finally, when she was nineteen, a diagnosis.

Cancer.

CHAPTER 2

KAHLILA

Kahlila was trying to process what was happening. She had been cleaning up after her school's end-of-year picnic. Then she started to feel weak, then her chest was pounding. Then she was on the ground.

An adult volunteer went to get her some water and a school police officer was hovering over her. The officer said, "Are you having a drug overdose?"

"No," she told the police officer, "I don't do drugs." Later, after a paramedic examined her, she learned she had passed out because she had forgotten to drink water and became dehydrated. But the police officer—who treated her like a stranger even though he was assigned to Kahlila's school and she saw him around all the time to and from classes or student government meetings—didn't seem to consider that option.

For a long time, Kahlila Williams didn't tell anyone what had happened. She didn't even tell her best friend, who had been at the event also but was too far to hear the officer's question.

The tangle of emotions Kahlila felt that day—confusion, anger, loss of safety—churned for a year. They churned as that same cop followed her on her way to school one day and asked who she was walking with (a friend) and what was in her cup (a Starbucks drink). They churned as she watched and admired adults who fought for social justice. "I just never thought I could do it. I couldn't see myself physically being in the fight [for justice] until maybe I was older."

They churned when Kahlila watched the video of a Minneapolis police officer dig his knee into George Floyd's neck and murder him, as her own junior year of high school was coming to a close. And those feelings fueled her into activism in the spring of 2020, when she learned that there was a group of students trying to get rid of school police.

Kahlila already understood some things about her school system, Los Angeles Unified School District (LAUSD). There was, after all, history baked into her own campus: Girls Academic Leadership Academy (GALA), a small all-girls school attached to a bigger school in the middle of Los Angeles. School leaders proudly told Kahlila and her classmates that GALA was the first all-girls school in the district, and the superintendent who pushed to open the school was the first Black woman to run LA Unified.[1]

Kahlila first connected with Students Deserve through Lindsay Herz, a resource specialist at her school who recognized that the teenager might want to use her voice beyond campus.[2] Students Deserve was, at the time, a group of student activists from about twenty Los Angeles schools (now there are more) who advocated for certain issues based on what each school needed. While the group is student-led, teachers across the district facilitate meetings, act as advisers and co-organizers, and, in some cases, recruit students. Lindsay didn't know what had happened to Kahlila in that park, but she did know that Kahlila had founded a Black Student Union at school, was involved in leadership, and seemed to want to make the school a better place.[3]

So Kahlila started to attend online meetings after school with Students Deserve. Student leaders, who she would soon call family, told her police officers are not the norm outside of their district. Wealthier, smaller, whiter school districts are less likely to put armed police in schools. But forty years before she entered the fight, the LA school board decided to make their own police department. That's why now, Kahlila and most other high school students in LA Unified, the second-biggest school district in the country, saw an officer on their campus every day.

In these conversations about organizing, Kahlila learned that other Black students also felt less safe with the police around. She was afraid of being targeted the way Black and brown people are outside of school and worried because police carry deadly weapons, like guns, and also painful ones, like pepper spray. Other students told her they had seen police pepper-spray their friends on campuses.

And she learned the statistics that made her fears warranted—a team of researchers from Kahlila's dream school, the University of California at Los Angeles, had found that police in Los Angeles schools arrest Black students at rates far higher and more disproportionate than other racial groups.[4] The police department is real, so the arrests are real, and the effect they have on kids' records and futures is real. That meant of every demographic in the entire school district, Black students like Kahlila were among the most likely to get arrested.

Leading came naturally to Kahlila, a member of her school's student government and an ambassador for the campus. And Students Deserve's style is to fold interested students into positions of responsibility and importance quickly. So as she and other students planned to rally outside school district headquarters the next week to encourage the school board to cut funding for school police, Kahlila jumped in with an idea. She wanted to create a message on the street that could draw participants in and would be visible from above when students stood on the letters, spelling out the message and showing their unity. The other students liked the idea and put Kahlila in charge of organizing.

One afternoon in late June, Lindsay and Kahlila drove downtown to the giant building that was the headquarters of Kahlila's school district. She had never been there before. She'd seen some of the other organizers in Zoom meetings, but this was Kahlila's first time meeting them, or anyone really, in person. The pandemic had kept everyone home for months.

Now all these adults, so nice and friendly and with more experience, were peppering Kahlila with questions as if she was in charge.

"Do you need any help?"

"The aerial photo was your idea."

"It's all in your hands."

"Where do you want the letters?"

"I don't know," Kahlila told them. *You're asking the wrong person*, she thought. The last time Kahlila had protested, she was only seven and still lived with her grandmother in Long Beach. Back then, Kahlila was protesting budget cuts that she said threatened to get her favorite teacher laid off at her elementary school. Even at that protest, she had delivered a speech and created a poster. A picture of her ran in the local newspaper. She was wearing a red shirt and looking down at a sign almost as big as her that said, "If you can read this, thank a teacher!"[5]

Now, as she stood outside the school district's headquarters, she wore a black shirt and camo pants with matching sneakers, the same outfit she'd worn on her sixteenth birthday—to help her feel comfortable but powerful. In this moment, though, she felt overwhelmed.

Lindsay stood by her side, suggested a spot Kahlila agreed to on the road where they could outline the message they'd agreed to: "DEFUND LASPD"—short for the Los Angeles School Police Department. While the traffic light was red, Lindsay then darted into a busy street to write letters in bright white chalk on the asphalt.

With the message complete, Kahlila started to finally relax after she met student organizers from other schools. They danced to a song by another teen activist called "Why We Need School Police?" laughing while it blasted from speakers as those very police stood by.

Why we need school police?
Yea I don't get it they causing the friction

I'm really not wit it. We need more counseling,
Nurses, the lunches, not meeting criteria
Why we need school police?[6]

Just when Kahlila was getting comfortable at her first protest in years, one of the teachers asked her to help get people into the street so they could get the rally started. The teacher pushed a bullhorn into Kahlila's hands.

What am I supposed to do with this? Kahlila thought, her hands shaking, her heart beating so hard she could feel it hitting her chest.

She started walking and racked her brain for the chants that she and other more experienced student organizers came up with the night before. Kahlila picked up the bullhorn and started the only one she could remember.

"Defund LASPD. We don't need no school police!"

A few cycles in, she realized she'd successfully brought a mass of people into the middle of the street. So she turned to them, and she told them her story.

CHAPTER 3

SONIA

S onia couldn't sing.

Or, she could—she could always sing, her voice was gorgeous. But she'd just gotten a notice from her choir leader that practice was canceled, unclear for how long, because of this sickness that was much deadlier than the flu. Apparently, singing could transmit the virus. It was March 2020.

Sonia Patel Banker had been a member of the prestigious Young Women's Chorus of San Francisco for seven years by then—close to half her life. Singing is what makes Sonia happy. She's good at it and, up until that point, she had never had to go without it. Sure, performing comes with its own pressures, but for Sonia it's also a beautiful release from school and stress and being a teenager. Music is her art, and she could not imagine life without it.

But in the spring of that year, Sonia couldn't go to school; she couldn't see her friends. It was frustrating and scary and made her anxious. Usually she could combat those feelings with choir. But that wasn't an option. Ever the planner, she looked for another outlet. She thought back to a few months before, when she'd held a bake sale to raise money for a youth program the choir had visited the summer before in South Africa.

Weeks after Sonia came home to San Francisco from that trip, she was thinking about the faded yellow walls and hard floors of the youth program in South Africa. As she and her choir were leaving, after exchanging songs with the kids there and delivering some donations, the director handed Sonia her card. "If you want to help more," she said, "get in touch." That trip to South Africa—each summer the choir goes to a different country to tour—was her first time understanding viscerally that many kids don't have the kind of access to important resources that she does.

As Sonia and her friends loaded the tour bus to leave Kliptown, South Africa, one of her friends suggested a fundraiser. They spent part of the bus ride scheming with two of Sonia's classmates to join in the effort. Planning had officially commenced.

That was July 2019. By September there was a plan. Sonia and her friends had come to it by asking themselves a series of questions: What about a bake sale during school lunch hours? What about selling sweets plus something savory for whoever doesn't feel like eating cafeteria food that day? What about showcasing a South African dessert at the bake sale? An email went out to the student body that included a video of the kids singing, information about the Kliptown Youth Program, from its website, and an appeal to buy sweet things:

> Their tutoring, athletic, and arts programs provide
> a life to the children of Kliptown not defined by
> survival, but by their ability to be active community

members, to have dreams, and most of all, to have hope for their futures.[1]

The weekend before, Sonia made four dozen chocolate chip cookies from an old family recipe. The house smelled like cookies, and it's possible (even likely) that fewer than forty-eight cookies made it to the sale since Sonia's mom and sister definitely stole some.

On a Monday in December the four choir girls set up a table in the Student Center by the lunch line, hoping to grab the lunch crowd at their hungriest. They sold out of the koeksisters (a traditional South African dessert) even though they were ten dollars each—and made a respectable profit from Sonia's cookies, donuts, and pork ribs. At the end of lunch, they counted the money—$364.70! Almost four times the amount the choir had raised that summer for donated supplies, and they'd seen firsthand the bags and bags of stuff that bought when converted to South African rand.

Excited, Sonia handed the cash over to her mother, a lawyer who was more equipped to figure out international money transfers. But then she felt . . . something off. Sometimes it can be hard to figure out exactly what you're feeling.

"What hit me is when that money left, when I was done, there was no resolution," Sonia said. She gave some money to an organization ten thousand miles away, one time, and she didn't know how they were going to use it or how helpful it would be or if it would impact children's outcomes in the long run. Answering those questions seemed like a lot to ask of a one-time donation. "It didn't feel complete to me."

This was a confusing feeling because Sonia had always asked people about their needs and then worked to deliver on them through volunteering or fundraising, as she'd been taught to do. She'd even won an award in eighth grade that was basically given to the school's most upstanding citizen. But she felt like that wasn't enough anymore. Sure, this fundraiser could help Kliptown. But because she lived in San Francisco, a place where people had vastly different access to resources, she began to wonder about the kids closer to home. Did they have access to art classes in their schools? Could their families pay for choir outside the school, like Sonia's? She didn't know. And she didn't know why she didn't know. And that was hard.

Ah, that was the feeling—dissatisfaction.

Now, at the height of the COVID pandemic, stuck in her room with its pale purple walls and the window taunting her with everything she couldn't do outside, Sonia confronted that feeling. She had heard that the American Civil Liberties Union (ACLU) had a summer camp for teens, and she was planning to attend it. Maybe they had some information about how to help people with art, and what people closer to her needed?

A few page clicks later, she saw it—exactly what she was looking for.

CRITICAL SELF-REFLECTION

What Sonia experienced, though she didn't identify it in the moment, was what some in movement work would call a period of critical self-reflection.

Like Sonia, Larissa Crawford traveled abroad as a teenager—to a girls' school in Ghana at sixteen, with her teacher. Larissa is the founder and managing director of Future Ancestor Services, a company that works to advance climate justice, decolonization, and anti-racism. Also like Sonia, she set up a fundraising drive in her city, then studied abroad in college, working with refugees and populations in need across the globe. As she did, Larissa began to wonder, *Why was I prioritizing international volunteer and humanitarian work and movement work when I wasn't investing that energy into where I come from and my own people?*

"As a visibly and historically racialized person, particularly being visibly Black and then carrying and existing as an Indigenous person, my existence has always been politicized," Larissa said. She began to think deeply about it and to research her roots, a practice that has helped shape the work she does today.

SONALI KOHLI: Why is critical self-reflection important?

LARISSA CRAWFORD: One learning that I really got from and really became aware of through this process was how important that is to know ourselves. How important it is to be rooted in our culture and our histories and our ancestry, so that when we are going and working in the global context, we aren't as susceptible to appropriating or taking on elements of someone else's experiences and cultures as our own in inappropriate ways.

SK: How can teenagers engage in that self-reflection?

LC: I've found so much feeling and understanding in myself and colonial legacies and how they've shaped my realities, and how they've shaped who I am through exploration of collective ancestry.

If you do have access to your biological family and you do have access to people who know your histories, I want to acknowledge that first this is a privilege. For many Indigenous peoples, many people who have gone through the foster care system, many people who have experienced separation of family, accessing your family history is not a reality, or it is made very, very, very difficult. So if you do have the privilege of accessing your family history and understanding how you came to where you live, if you have access to understanding who your ancestors were, who your biological ancestors were and what they did, I strongly recommend taking your time to have those conversations with your family to develop a deeper understanding of yourself and to expand your understanding of self to include those that have come before you to make you who you are today.

For many reasons, I didn't have access to our direct family history. We always knew we are Métis with Cree ancestry, but we never really had the opportunity to understand well—what family members, where did they come from? Not until later in life when we started having those more explicit conversations and we started investing hours and hours and hours into researching and tracing those family lineages. With regards to my Jamaican ancestry, this isn't possible for many reasons. The Transatlantic Slave Trade had many explicit practices that destroyed our connection to our lineage, to our family. And so in absence of this, I've sought to understand that collective ancestry of transatlantic enslaved people, of those who were brought to Jamaica, and pursuing that research of what happened in Jamaica, where did they come from?

I always encourage this exploration of an expanded understanding of self. So for me when I think of self, yes, I think of my bodily needs, my independent means, and I think about my intrinsic love for my body and for myself, but I also understand myself and self-care as also meaning the well-being of my daughter, as also being the well-being of my community. I understand self as my relationship to Earth and the existence and well-being of Earth. I do it with a simple word map and I do a little drawing of me and I start just putting down words and things that I understand as self that makes me who I am.

I highly encourage this way of reflecting on your role in activist spaces and movements, because this is a way that we can go into those spaces and engage and relate to one another.

SK: If you're someone who's a young person who's getting started in this work, how do you know that the way that you're contributing is inappropriate and/or unethical?

LC: First and foremost, recognize that what we're doing is not new and that it exists within a legacy. If we are to contribute to activist movements and spaces, we have a responsibility to understand where we fit into those legacies. And so that can start with seeking out different books and simple Googling: the history of the movement and the history of this kind of harm. It doesn't have to be complicated. It doesn't have to be in a classroom. It can be in a classroom, it can be in a cool program or fellowship, but it doesn't have to be. This is one of the quickest ways to avoid leading with ego.

We can't exclude the value that elders and people who've been doing this work for twenty, thirty years have. They may not use all the right language that we use, they may not be totally up to date on how to use the technology that we rely on, but we cannot uphold those barriers. Because if we are not engaging in intergenerational collaboration, then we are doing harm to our movement. We are doing harm to our activism.

And then finally, accepting that you're going to mess up. And again, this is where we really have to let go of leading with ego. We have to accept that we are going to mess up. We are likely going to be called out for messing up, and there are different ways that people are called out. Yes, it may be done publicly. Yes, it may be done with an angry tone. It may not be done with the language that you appreciate. It may be done very lovingly and to the side, it may be done very compassionately. However it's done, we need to accept that this may and will happen. And once we accept that, and once we get kind of comfortable with at least the discomfort of being wrong, then we hold space to change our behavior or to at least reflect deeper on our behavior and actions so that when we move forward, we are at less risk of causing harm.

1. Nalleli, Kahlila, and Sonia all see or experience wrongdoing and want to make a situation better for themselves or others. Have you experienced someone being treated badly, including yourself? What did you do?

2. What is an area of your life in which you could explore critical self-reflection?

3. Who is someone you could talk to or a resource you could find to understand your legacy?

PART 2

KNOW YOUR STORY

We realize the importance of our voices when we are silenced.

—MALALA YOUSAFZAI,
global education rights activist[1]

CHAPTER 4

NALLELI

Nalleli remembers her childhood home as full and happy and stacked with four generations of love. Two of her great-grandparents, her grandmother, her mother, three siblings, and Nalleli—a household of eight—crammed themselves into their small South Los Angeles apartment. It was always loud in the best way. The closeness is why she still talks to all her siblings every day.

"I'm a very proud daughter of immigrants. I'm a very proud product of a single mother," Nalleli tells anyone who asks about her heritage and upbringing. She was born in Bellflower, California, and is proud to be Colombian and Mexican and American. "I'm a strong woman because of my mom and seeing that she always gave me that example in life."

As Nalleli has grown up, she's come to under-stand that there's a lot of factors in her own life and in society that had to come together for her to be in the very specific position of getting poisoned by an oil well across from her home. Los Angeles is a sprawling county with one very large city and a bunch of small ones. Nalleli lived in the city. It has always been, and remains, segregated—people of different races and who have more or less money than each other live in very different parts of the city.[1] Immigrants like Nalleli's mom often come to Los Angeles without much money, so they look for apartments they can afford. Those neighborhoods tend to have worse air quality, more sickness, and a lower life expectancy.[2] There are nonprofit groups, like Esperanza Community Housing, that buy land or buildings and rent their apartments to families for a lower rent. Nalleli's mom worked for Esperanza, and they lived in one of the nonprofit's apartment buildings.

The homes in those areas were more likely to be exposed to chemicals that companies use to extract as much oil as they can but also cause the symptoms Nalleli and her neighbors were feeling. Early on, a *Los Angeles Times* reporter who from the start covered the community activism and harm from the oil wells, became one of Nalleli's favorite journalists to talk to. In one of his many news stories about the site, he explained what the oil company had done that could be causing some of the symptoms: "Allenco bought the oil production facility in 2009, and used hydrochloric acid and phosphoric acid to unplug some of the wells. Within a year production jumped more than 400%, from 4,178 barrels to 21,239 barrels in 2010."[3] Before they bought the facility, the wells had been idle for more than a decade. After the purchase, neighbors made more than 250 complaints in three years.[4]

These chemicals, the reporter noted, are used in a process called "acidizing" to clean out a well by dissolving rocks and other underground formations that are in the way of the company getting oil out of the ground.[5] It's not possible to know exactly what methods and chemicals AllenCo used because they didn't have to report every process and chemical. But hydrochloric acid alone causes many of the health issues, including asthma, that Nalleli and her family—her mother and grandmother developed asthma—experienced during her childhood.

"Environmental racism is if someone wants to open an oil well, and they were looking to drill in [the overwhelmingly Latino and lower-income neighborhood of] Wilmington . . . they would approve them without basically even reading them, just green stamps, green stamps. And if I were then trying to open a well in predominantly a white community, for example, Culver City or Beverly Hills, then I would be told to make sure I only operate during the hours of nine to five when people typically aren't home. I would have to make sure that there are silent drills, I would have to make sure that special filters are put up, I would have to ensure that the outside is beautified with mosaics and tiles and flowers, and I could only use five oil wells. In my community, AllenCo had 21 oil wells and they would produce an average of 80 barrels of crude oil a day. That's environmental racism," Nalleli told an environmental podcast years later. "It's seeing our community as less than. It's seeing our zip code, our socioeconomic status, or ethnicity as deeming us as less valuable. And that's not true, nor is it right."[6]

Then there's the oil piece of it. The archdiocese of Los Angeles—the local arm of the Catholic church—owns the land that AllenCo was drilling on. That the church rented the land to AllenCo and made $735,000 on it in just two and a half years was especially disappointing to Nalleli, who was raised Christian and went to Catholic schools.[7] It seemed to her that letting people use land in a way that harmed others was not a great application of the church's values.

Plus, oil companies have a lot of political power because they have a lot of money and are responsible for so many of the things we consume. So even though Nalleli and her neighbors were the ones local politicians and authorities were supposed to serve, the activists weren't able to get the site shut down, even when it was clear that they were suffering because of the site's presence.

Nalleli was hopeful when she learned the church owned the land. She's a spiritual person who believes in God and in the lessons the church tries to impart about doing good. Surely the people who were the stewards of those lessons would want to help the communities where so many of their members came from, once they knew the harm being done, she thought.

Nalleli was wrong. Again and again, when journalists would contact the archdiocese for comment, they would give the same nonresponse, deferring responsibility to the people leasing the land.

It usually read like this statement the archdiocese gave to the *Los Angeles Times* in 2013: "We take the residents' concerns seriously. We are examining our lease with Allenco to ensure their operations are in compliance with our agreement. We continue to work with all involved parties to see that health standards are being met at the site."[8]

Pretty soon Nalleli and her mom had the statement from the archdiocese memorized. "It's like copy and paste at this point," Nalleli said, just switch out the publication they're talking to.

And she was incredibly disappointed.

"It's because I know what they teach us that I know they're being hypocrites," she said. "You can't sit a group of youth down and educate us about God and God's creation and tell us that we need to love our neighbor and love God's creation and treat others the way we want to be treated and give back to the church, but you're gonna choose to poison us to get a few bucks in?"

CHAPTER 5

KAHLILA

"**H**ide, hide!" her mother urgently told ten-year-old Kahlila, as they heard footsteps on gravel in the alley. Kahlila's mom had already kept her home from school that week, afraid after a social worker was constantly sniffing around campus. Now, it seemed, police were coming home to find her.

Kahlila rushed to the bathroom, where there was an inconspicuous storage space no one used. She stuffed herself inside and put the laundry basket on top. Police searched the house, walking past her to check the shower, as she tried to make herself smaller. Eventually, unable to find her, they left.

Let's rewind for a moment to Kahlila's first encounter with police. That happened years before this one, when she was so young that it might be one of her first memories. She was sitting in the bathroom, watching her biological mother—then just "Mom"—get ready for the day. Kahlila used to love watching her mom swipe bold, colorful makeup on her lips and eyes. She was distinctive from everyone else. More exciting. Then there was a banging on the front door, and loud noises. The door hit little Kahlila, about three years old at the time, as police barged into the bathroom and arrested her mother in front of her.

Kahlila's mother was incarcerated for almost two years after that, two of Kahlila's early childhood years. Kahlila still doesn't know why, or whether her mom was in prison, jail, or some other form of law enforcement detention during that time. For some of that time she lived with her doting grandmother and uncle in Long Beach, California. She discovered her mother was back when one day her uncle loaded everyone in the car. She dozed off on the drive, and "when I woke up, my mom was there," she said.

After that, her biological mom was in and out of her life. She mostly lived with her grandmother and would see her mother in between or during her mom's abusive romantic relationships. After Kahlila's grandmother died when she was nine, though, she had to live with her mom and her mother's boyfriend. And while she grieved her grandma's death, she also had to help her mom navigate the real world—as a nine-year-old.

"I really was the adult of the household," she said—helping her mom find the online portals for bills, figuring out how to continue to pay the rent on a lease that was in a dead woman's name, watching her rely financially on a man who mistreated her because after incarceration it is so hard to find work. These are the kinds of memories that resurfaced later—that she processed as she grew and eventually realized were not fair to her or her mother.

"At points I saw my mother trying and she wasn't given the resources to really help herself, and she didn't know enough either," Kahlila said.

This all led to Kahlila hiding in the bathroom. Kahlila suspects that her neighbor, after hearing loud arguments, was the one who called police or made complaints about her care—and she doesn't blame her. It was a bad situation. Kahlila had seen the bruises on her mother. She worried. But Kahlila did not realize that this call meant police were still looking for her, and that if she dialed 9-1-1 for any reason, she would be ripped away from her family.

On the day her baby sister was born, that's exactly what happened.

Kahlila had recently turned ten and was with her aunt in Long Beach while her mother was in the hospital giving birth. Kahlila had fought with her cousin, the kind of trivial fight kids have, and was angry with her aunt for not believing her. She stalked off, saying she was going to call the police—she wanted to go to her mom, she wanted to meet her little sister—police were supposed to be helpful, right? They had cars, they could reunite her with her mom and the new baby.

Kahlila dialed.

Police came.

They did not take her to her mother. Or her sister. Or any other family member.

Kahlila spent the rest of the day and the night in police cars and in a processing center, and then in a stranger's home. The police put Kahlila in the custody of Child Protective Services. There was no family they could place her with—there seemed to be a case open against her mother. Her grandmother had died, her aunt was the one she complained about when she called, and her uncle had an open, unrelated case.

Instead Kahlila spent most of the next year in foster and group homes. First in Montclair, at least an hour from her mom; then to a group home in Altadena, also an hour from her mom.

Kahlila threw herself into schoolwork—it was an escape to learn and she soaked everything in, constantly asking questions and getting good grades. She needed a distraction from worrying about her mom and sister and grieving her grandmother, who had been cremated just a month before she was taken from her family. At the first foster home, school was also a break from her roommate, who was older than Kahlila and made her feel uncomfortable, sometimes even throwing large objects at her.

"There was just a lot of emotions going around and school kind of gave me a way to get away from all of that and focus on something else," Kahlila said.

Years later, she'd tell the adults who make decisions about kids' fates in Los Angeles about how important a safe school environment was to her well-being.

At the group home in Altadena, her moments of freedom were diluted—the kids were homeschooled, and the only out was the Boys and Girls Club in the afternoons. The girls in the home could earn computer privileges, and that allowed Kahlila to talk to her family. She could then ask her uncle and other family members about her mom and sister. There were tiny bright spots too—watching Fourth of July fireworks at the Rose Bowl, meeting her first boyfriend (the relationship consisted of passing notes and lasted a whole week) at the Boys and Girls Club, and playing laser tag for the first time.

But it wasn't a stable environment. "It depends on what day it was," Kahlila said. "I would wake up sometimes in the middle of the night and my roommate would be just staring at me." The next roommate rifled through Kahlila's stuff, found the notepad where she kept her passwords, and contacted Kahlila's family, pretending to be her.

On July 16, 2014, Kahlila met her new foster mom, Vashawnne, a preschool teacher. She lived in a two-bedroom apartment in Jefferson Park, a neighborhood in the middle of Los Angeles. Jefferson Park is a historically Black neighborhood, and students there are zoned into Los Angeles Unified schools, which Kahlila started attending. Her new foster mother had strong family connections—her own mother lived next door, and her sister was down the street. They coincidentally had the same last name—Williams.

Kahlila finally had her own room, and she was the only foster child. Soon she would feel safe, healthy, and loved. Soon she'd start calling Vashawnne "Mom," and this apartment, "home."

CHAPTER 6

SONIA

Sonia had never been without. She knew her grandfather grew up in a village in India, that her grandparents, who immigrated to the United States, had worked hard to build the foundation for the comfort she and her family experienced.

On Grandparents and Special Friends Day in seventh grade, Sonia gave a speech to her school about her grandfather. She stood in front of a somber wood podium in her school uniform, glancing down at her paper every so often while alternately making eye contact with the audience.

She told the kids and teachers of the farming village in the state of Gujarat where her grandfather and his five siblings shared a small home with their parents and grandparents and how the siblings left their school's dirt floors and the worn wooden writing slates to tend to animals and crops under a hot sun. The crowd let out a collective rumble when she told them her grandfather took the college entrance exam with a typhoid fever of 103.5, and politely "ooh"-ed, impressed, when she told them he came first in the exam and then went on to perch in the bookstore near his college where the owner let him study from books for free because he couldn't afford to buy them. He made it through medical school, she told them, applied to residencies in the United States, borrowed money for a plane ticket, then worked long hours to support his family back home as well as Sonia's grandmother, mom, and aunt. He even missed his second daughter's birth to save actress Elizabeth Taylor's life after she choked on a chicken bone while visiting his town. He instilled the need to help people into all three of his children, Sonia said—that's why her mom became a public interest lawyer and her aunt and uncle became doctors.

"How was my grandfather able to come to the United States? How was he able to survive with only eight dollars in his pocket? How did he become one of the top gastroenterology specialists in Houston? He was able to do this through his determination, persistence, and hope," Sonia said to her fellow students.

When you're a descendant of that, "you don't know quite how to make their sacrifice worthwhile," Sonia said. It's an intense pressure—sometimes self-imposed, sometimes implied, sometimes imparted in pieces of well-meaning advice about what to do with your life.

Sonia loved living in foggy San Francisco, but she missed the fresh snow that comes with the bite of the East Coast cold she got as a little girl in Boston, before her parents moved with her and her little sister to California. When she wants to feel most at home, she retreats to her grandparents' home in Houston, where even though there are enough rooms for everyone to sleep on their own, she shares a room with her sister so they can talk and laugh into the night.

For someone who revels that much in memory, it's hard when you can't get together with friends to make new memories. So while it was difficult in 2020 to deal with online classes and not seeing her friends, it was even harder to miss out on choir practice—the perfect outlet for her introversion. Sonia's mom, Sejal, gave her the idea of channeling her passion for singing into helping people. Sejal didn't realize Sonia would stay so close to the family business of law.

This time, though, she didn't want to hold a bake sale or make a one-time donation or do some community service for the sake of bolstering her college application. Those experiences left her feeling like she wasn't doing enough to honor the privilege she had, a privilege not shared by the older generations of her family. She knew she was lucky, that she had a lot more as a teen than her parents and grandparents and plenty more than others around her. That comes with guilt for Sonia. But after the bake sale, she felt ready to turn the guilt into action.

"I realized, I want to do more than feel bad about it," Sonia said. "I want to use the advantages I have."

She wanted to know which people needed help and how she could help them. She wanted to understand an issue. That summer Sonia was supposed to go to an ACLU camp that her friend at school had told her about. *With COVID in full force, who knew if that would happen*, she thought, *but maybe that was a place to start looking for folks who needed help?*

Thinking the ACLU of Northern California's website might be a good place to start, she clicked around on the site. Scrolling to the bottom of a page, she saw a digital flier—the ACLU's Southern California chapter seemed to be trying to get access to arts education to kids across the state. There was an email address at the bottom of the page for Amir Whitaker, a lawyer and advocate. Sonia didn't know just how many schools were without arts education. Sure, she went outside of school for choir, but her school had plenty of other art options. She also didn't know that legally, every school in California was supposed to provide arts education to kids. This could be the deeper issue she could help with, she thought.

A common experience of being raised by successful parents of successful immigrants is that you develop a certain need for independence—a desire to prove to yourself, your family, and the world that you can do things on your own and a desire to make them proud. Sonia could have asked her mom to make an introduction to someone at the ACLU. But she didn't. Instead, in April 2020 she emailed Amir, the organizer and lawyer who is a mentor to dozens of Southern California youth. He was about to become her mentor, too.

Amir's childhood veered so far from Sonia's it seemed unimaginable that they experienced the same America. Amir grew up in New Jersey in the 1980s and '90s. In his autobiography, he wrote of his sophomore year in high school, "The only reason I made it this far in school is because I force myself to go every morning . . . well, most mornings. No alarm clock. No cheerful parents calling from the living room to wake me up. No breakfast on the table like on TV."[1]

Amir loved his parents, who taught him to be honest, respectful, and kind, and to stay away from the drugs they themselves had become addicted to.[2] Both his parents experienced addiction and incarceration, often leaving him to care for himself, which led him to sell dope and crack—which he refers to as "that poison"—when he was Sonia's age. At first, he sold drugs so he could eat and buy new clothes for school, but he didn't stop. He was expelled from high school, arrested, and imprisoned, released on probation, and sold drugs again after he finished high school and started community college.

He stopped dealing and returned to school, where after twelve years he earned five degrees to make him an academic doctor and a lawyer. Through it all, he was always working with kids, and art always held him down—he drew his friend's first tattoo and one of his own, learned guitar in community college, wrote poetry, and joined several bands as a student at Rutgers University. During college, he substitute-taught in his old school district; and while a graduate student in educational psychology at USC, he worked on college prep with high school students in the same Los Angeles neighborhood where Nalleli would start getting horrible nosebleeds just a few years later. In 2012, while at University of Miami's law school, he founded Project Knucklehead—an organization with the goal to "create programs for youth to help them stay in school and avoid incarceration."[3] By the time Sonia met Amir, Project Knucklehead was using art as an avenue to meet that goal.

Before Sonia met Amir and before he was at the ACLU, Amir had already spent a few years fighting for student rights through his work at the UCLA Civil Rights Project, bringing to light Los Angeles schools' uneven enforcement of "random searches" of students.[4]

All Sonia knew so far was that Amir was a big-shot ACLU lawyer working on getting access to arts funding for California youth. Four days after she sent the email, Amir responded—"I was so excited, it was like hearing from a celebrity"—and they scheduled a phone call. Sonia showed up with a pink sticky note covered in questions, expecting him to refer her to some articles to read. Instead, Amir asked Sonia all about her life, her work, her passions and what she wanted. He told her about the zine that arts justice fellows with the ACLU of Southern California had made. She seemed passionate and talented, he said, and our last arts justice fellow just left. Would you be interested in taking their spot?

BUILDING YOUR ARTISTIC TOOLBOX

By Sonia Patel Banker

Art is a great catalyst for change because it allows us to reimagine the world and form questions about its most pressing challenges. This Q&A interview explores how youth can use art as a way to engage in advocacy work. I talked to Yareli Arreola, who was the programs manager for the In-Schools team at 826 Valencia, a nonprofit organization that helps students develop their writing skills.

> **SONIA BANKER:** I imagine that you have worked with students who come into 826, and don't consider themselves writers or don't consider themselves artists. How do you, as someone who works directly with these youth, help them find their inner creative, help them discover that voice?
>
> **YARELI ARREOLA:** I think it starts with just building community with the students. I put a big emphasis and focus on building that trust and community in the classroom so that they can then feel comfortable sharing [their] writing. Writing is a very personal thing. It's often hard. A lot of students that I work with are second-language learners,

I think it also helps that I'm a second-language learner myself, and I share similar identities with students. I'm an immigrant, first generation. English wasn't my first language, [and I] also grew up in a very similar environment that these students are in. And I think that this helped a lot in building that trust, building that community. It's always fun to be like, "Oh, I don't know how to say this word" or "I have a typo because English is my second language," like it's not a big deal. And that also, I think, builds that trust for students to be like, "Oh, this is like my instructor who also sometimes struggled with English or doesn't know how to spell a word." So then that builds connection. Building trust within the community is really important.

SB: That's amazing. I think that synergy between art and social justice is really important because it's celebrating this possibility of a more equitable, just, creative, imaginative world.

YA: I always say, "Joy is what moves us forward." Joy, laughter, love, all those things. There has to be this middle ground where, yes, we're fighting, but also, I'm honoring the joy that I'm experiencing right now. Continue to fight, because if I don't have joy, I don't have motivation to keep going forward.

SB: If you were to break it down, how would you say that students found their awareness through the program [826], and how can we use that as a guide for other youth?

YA: When it comes to the actual writing process, it often starts with just listing experiences they want to focus on. It starts with a brainstorm, it starts with really thinking deeply about, What is your ultimate message for your audience? What is the call to action that you want to give to people? And then it's just really trusting the process and being honest with it. Writing is very vulnerable. But it's believing in your voice, it's believing that your voice deserves to be heard, and that there are people who want to hear what you have to say. It's trusting that there's an audience for this as well. And then ultimately, revision: getting whatever message you want checked out by your peers, by a tutor, by anyone that you're working with. But I think the biggest one is, again, trusting your voice, and knowing that it deserves to be heard.

SB: When students don't feel like they have the outlet to find people who trust their voices, how can they do that? When they want to share that voice, but they really feel like they can't find the people to do that with?

YA: I think this is where social media comes in handy. I really do believe in the power of social media. I generally believe communities can be formed online. I think finding your people in real life can be very isolating, especially if you're a queer kid of color, for example, which, myself included. Online is where I first found my community, online is where I found people who were my age, growing up in Mexican households where it was not okay to exist in the ways that we do. I think it's about trusting your message and also just being brave enough to share a little, and if it doesn't go good or if you're not comfortable, you don't have to do it again. But if you by chance, you [find] one person, right? Oftentimes, they are people who want to build community that are looking for similar people to connect with.

SB: What would you say about artists who can use their creative passion to fuel social change? Where do you think they would start and what skill set would [they] need to do that?

YA: I think ultimately, it starts with the people you're directly around. It starts with having conversations that are often taboo and hard to have. It starts with challenging any wrong that you see around you. And thinking about who you center yourself with or who you align yourself with. Are these people living up to your morals and values that you have? Do you share those ideals with the same people? Because being an artist or being an organizer or anything, you need community in every part of your life, as an adult, as a young person. You need to have people who are on your side and are ready to stand in that fight with you.

SB: If someone who's completely brand-new to all of this is thinking, "I want to get into art for the first time, and artivism specifically," what advice do you have for those people?

YA: I would say just start. With creatives, we are all borrowers. We borrow ideas and make them our own. We borrow images and transform them into something that directly reflects what we want to say. So never be afraid to use inspiration from someone else. I think there's already so many people who might have said something you want to say, so how can you make that your own? I think art is an intimidating process, but just knowing that there are people who want to hear your voice and will give you a platform to share your ideas. So really, just get started. Make a Pinterest board, find quotes, use prompts online, take templates of things, and make them your own.

DISCUSSION QUESTIONS

1. Have you ever used art to make a point or bring about change? How did you do it?
2. What would be in your artists' toolbox?
3. If not art, what is in your toolbox? How do you think about your own story?

PART 3

FOOTPRINTS ON THE MOON

You must find a way to get in the way, you must find a way to get into trouble. Good trouble, necessary trouble . . . that is your calling. That is your mission. That is your moral obligation. That is your mandate. Get out there and do it. Get in the way.

—JOHN LEWIS, United States congressman and civil rights leader[1]

CHAPTER 7

NALLELI

The phone rang late one night in fall 2013, the night before Nalleli's sister was getting married. As twelve-year-old Nalleli spooned her caldo de papa, her mom, Monic, answered the phone and then stepped away, beginning to cry. "Tell us!" the family urged.

Monic hung up and turned to them—"AllenCo is closing," she said. Nalleli remembers jumping up and down and screaming. She rushed to the window and opened it even though it was a cold night, breathing in air she knew wouldn't be tainted.[1]

Finally, they felt the payoff of years of work convincing local environmental authorities to listen to them and test the air for toxic fumes, which got the attention of the *Los Angeles Times*, which got the attention of US Senator Barbara Boxer, who demanded an investigation from the US Environmental Protection Agency, whose officers experienced on one single tour many of the same symptoms Nalleli had been feeling.[2] After that, AllenCo had agreed to stop its operations during the investigation.[3]

But AllenCo wasn't planning to leave the site forever. They said they would make necessary changes to keep neighbors safe and then reopen with city oversight.

When someone slashed the tires and broke the windows of the family car earlier in the year, Nalleli and her family thought, "Oh well, bad luck"—this kind of incident certainly wasn't rare where they lived. Then about four months after AllenCo stopped operations, the family came home one day to find their home had been broken into. Pair that with the car and the fact that more than once a man bumped into Nalleli's mom in the street and ominously told her, "You have to stay quiet"—Nalleli was scared. To this day they can't be sure who, if anyone, targeted them. But the groups they spoke out against most were oil companies and the archdiocese.

Nalleli doesn't know the name of the man who threatened her mother—"I didn't want to know," she said. "I wanted to hate the action, not a person." But her life changed drastically one spring afternoon. She was sitting in seventh-grade English class, working on a vocabulary book and discussing her friend's upcoming trip to Las Vegas. It was a very exciting discussion because the friend would be visiting M&M's World and promised to bring everyone a present. Nalleli asked for a stuffed green M&M toy. Everyone knows the green one is the sauciest.

Then they heard, "Nalleli for early dismissal" over the intercom. A little confused but mostly happy to be leaving school early, Nalleli made her way to the office. Her mom and principal were waiting, and they ushered her into the principal's car—not a place Nalleli had been before. That's where they broke the news. Nalleli was leaving her classmates. She would not be able to return to this school. She wouldn't be getting the green M&M toy, and she wouldn't be able to tell her friends why.

They said she was going into witness protection. Tears welled and began to spill.

"What do you mean?" Nalleli said. She doesn't remember who spoke next, her mother or principal or both.

But one of them told her, "We have to go into this program. We're going to go interview at two different schools right now to see if they accept you." Remaining at this school, they told her, is "a safety hazard for you at this point, and also for the other kids."

At the time, and to a degree still, all Nalleli understood about the situation was what her mother told her—that detectives thought that Nalleli and her mother were in danger because of the pattern of incidents, and because they were well known in the community for the work they were doing against oil drilling. The other factors—who broke in, whether they were connected to the man on the street who brushed past her mother with a threat—all remain fuzzy. They didn't make sense then, nor do they now.

As usual, Nalleli and her older sister questioned what their experience would be like based on the Disney Channel. Would a black car follow them around, like in the movie *Princess Protection Program*? Would someone in a dark suit be in every restaurant they went to, protecting them? No on both counts.

Instead, police told Nalleli and her mom that they were allowed to move to one of five cities within a small radius of their current home. They had twenty minutes to pack what they could, with one officer inside and another outside. A few days later they came back for another fifteen-minute sprint to grab what they could.

At the time everyone was using Kik, an app, to message. Nalleli had to delete hers. She effectively ghosted her friends. Her new, two-bedroom apartment was on the third floor of a building with an elevator—her first and only apartment with an elevator to this day. Where their home used to be full of raucous, happy noises and siblings, it was now just Nalleli, one of her sisters, and their mom.

When the loneliness drove Nalleli to be rebellious and log into Kik, she'd see messages from her friends:

"Hey, where are you?"

"When are you coming back to school? I miss you."

She'd log out without responding and return to her new life in her new school, where people would learn quickly that she was an activist, but they didn't learn why or how difficult it was.

"At my new school, I was just Nalleli who moved to a 'better area,' and that was that."

When you're a kid in witness/victim protection, all the adults around you drill hard that your existence is a secret, and exposing it could cost your life. For a kid without the context of exactly who was targeting her family, and how, and why, that lesson doesn't fade quickly.

At first, she asked her mom, "Okay, how long can I not talk to my friends? A week? A month?"

"Much longer," her mom said, without an end date in sight.

"When can I go back to my school?" Nalleli would ask. Her mom gently reminded her that they had talked about this—she couldn't go back.

Eventually Nalleli learned "how to adapt to my ever-changing life without asking questions about it."

One morning about two or three years in—she's tried to compress that period of time in her memory—she was eating cereal when her mother told her they were being released from witness protection. Nalleli had never felt the fear she did in that moment. "No!" she told her mom. "Tell them they need to give it to us for another year." The thoughts swirled, out of control—what if someone was waiting to attack her or her family?

Nalleli's mom, tender as always, reminded her that nothing bad had happened to them in years, and they weren't going to go back to the community they lived in. They'd stay in the apartment they were in, and Nalleli would finish school here. The difference was that police wouldn't be keeping tabs on them, and if they did have to go to their old neighborhood for an action or photo as they sometimes did, an officer would not be there to keep watch.

For a decade after she was pulled out of that seventh-grade class, Nalleli was afraid to share this part of her story, worried that whoever sent the first bunch to intimidate her family would send more people to hurt them. She and her mother stayed in witness protection for around two years. But she didn't tell most of her friends what had happened until long afterward.

CHAPTER 8

KAHLILA

Kahlila spoke at her first school board meeting in late June 2020, when the LAUSD Board of Education was deciding whether to cut the school police budget. She rallied outside district headquarters with her new co-organizers and mentors as they chanted, waved posters, and amped each other up for the day ahead.

She then went inside the imposing building and addressed the board members. The mostly white group of seven people made decisions about how to spend money in a district where most children are Black and brown. She told her peers outside, and then the board members inside, about the school police officer assigned to her school.

When she introduced herself as a rising senior, her voice was soft, timid even. But as she began to talk about the end-of-year picnic her sophomore year, where she passed out from dehydration and woke up to the school police officer asking if she had consumed drugs, her voice grew stronger and more passionate.

"Instead of getting assistance I needed by a nurse, a school police officer was there when I regained consciousness," she told them. "Instead of getting help, I was accused of having a drug overdose."[1] She was referencing the fact that Los Angeles high schools did not all have nurses on campus every day, but they did have police on campus every day. The money on 435 uniformed officers could, in her opinion, be spent so much better.

When Kahlila speaks to powerful figures, she doesn't just repeat the lines she's heard from adults around her. Instead, she follows the thought experiment all the way through. She asked the board—so what if she *was* abusing drugs at that picnic? Would a police officer be most helpful in that situation, or should schools spend that money on someone with more expertise in substance abuse? "Police instill more fear into our students' day-to-day lives. Hiring a drug counselor would provide a real assistance to students who need it. That's why funding toward nurses, school counselors, [therapists], and ethnic studies is what we need."

Kahlila told the board that day that she used to look forward to school as an escape from a "bad home life." She said she considered herself lucky that her third foster home was the one she'd been in for the last six years, where she felt safe and cared for. But that's not a reality for many kids.

Kahlila explained that she wanted school to be a safe and stable place for her and for kids like her. That's what drove her to this work, and police don't make her feel safe or stable. They represent a justice system that jailed both her biological parents and that assumes the worst in her.

Her voice was polite, formal, but strong.

"Don't wait another week, don't wait another month," she told them. "We as Black youth need action now. Stop pushing off our needs as if we're not a priority to you. As school board members, your number one priority is safety, but school police don't make students feel safe."

Kahlila spoke about two hours into the meeting, during the "public comment" section. Only one school board member was actually there, wearing a mask and gloves. The rest participated from their homes or offices and had live images of them projected onto a giant screen behind the dais. The president of the board had to be told repeatedly to unmute himself. The youngest board member nursed her baby. About six hours after Kahlila first spoke—after dozens more comments from students, parents, and activists encouraging the school board to show their values through their money allocation, after school police officers spoke to defend their profession, after the superintendent gave an update on coronavirus school closures and district staff delved into some of the details of the school budget—the school board finally came to the amendment that Kahlila and her new colleagues were there for.

Mónica Garcia, the only present school board member, introduced a motion to amend the budget they were voting on. She proposed cutting $35 million from the school police budget and reallocating that money to Black student achievement. That's half of the entire budget for school police, even though it's less than 1 percent of the cost to run the whole district.[2]

Usually with decisions like this, everyone knows what they're doing before the actual vote. They might talk and argue, but few minds are changed in the moment. On this day, though, there was negotiating on the virtual dais. More than one board member expressed their shame and desire to do better, but they weren't all willing to slash the police force by that much. After more than an hour of discussion, they came to enough of an agreement for a majority to vote.

Kahlila watched in suspense, surrounded by activists, young and old, some of whom had been fighting for this kind of reduction in policing for a decade, with incremental wins: When Kahlila was ten, school police returned military-grade weapons from the federal government.[3] When she was fifteen, the school board phased out random searches, which police weren't supposed to be involved in but often were.[4] The hope was that in time they would whittle down the power and force of the police until they were abolished completely. There were the fellow youth from Students Deserve and folks from the many organizations who had been working toward this goal for years. One was Amir from Project Knucklehead and the ACLU.

Before he became Sonia's mentor, and one of Kahlila's, Amir had been working with youth who were impacted by "random searches," understanding how their experiences were not actually random and helping them advocate for themselves to the school board.[5] Amir understood that art looked like many different things and that throughout history activists had used words to stir feelings and action in the same way a painter or singer would. To him, Kahlila's speaking presence was its own form of art, as much as Sonia's singing. After police murdered George Floyd in 2020 and the uprisings began that summer, Project Knucklehead received a big donation that Amir used to set up a fellowship program for California youth artists and activists. He would soon ask Kahlila if she'd like to be a part of the fellowship. Not long after that, he'd start calling her "Scraps" because she was little but fierce.[6]

The school board voted to cut $25 million from the $70 million school police budget that night. It wasn't 50 percent, but it was more than a third of the total budget. The next day, another win—the Los Angeles schools police chief was stepping down amid all these cuts.[7] They were well on their way to dismantling school police.

FIND YOUR MOVEMENT

By Kahlila Williams

Baba Akili is a longtime civil and human rights activist. He was born in the segregated South, during the height of Jim Crow, where the laws, customs, and practices reinforced Black people's second-class status in America and sought to erase you as a person.

I met Baba Akili at a Jackie Lacey protest in 2020, and I was inspired by his speech and the work he has done. To see someone who has been in this work for over fifty years was so inspirational because I didn't even believe I could do the work I am doing. But seeing it's possible to devote my life to this work and still be going fifty-plus years later pushes me to keep going.

From his experiences he developed three principles:

1. People make a difference if you go to them; it's not enough to have a good idea and keep it in this room.
2. The essence of democracy is inclusion and participation. We live in the richest country in the world, so we can have a just, fair, and equitable society.

3. Four conditions that I've observed that Black people face: white supremacy, institutional racism, individual bigotry, and mass denial. Based upon those conditions, Black folks have continued to struggle. Black folks have to continue to advance and Black people have to continue to raise ourselves and raise our interest and advance the kind of changes that we want to see for ourselves, our families, and for future generations, like you.

KAHLILA WILLIAMS: What is organizing/movement work?

BABA AKILI: My definition of organizing is getting people together around their own behalf in their own beliefs based on their own interest, getting them to accept responsibility for making the change by doing the work and building an organization that protects, promotes, and defends your interest. Recognizing that people have power no matter what we have been taught to believe. When you bring people together, they have power to make change. You have to see the conditions, understand the conditions, and accept what can be done as an organizer.

Organizing is about bringing people in and helping them realize their capacity and then use that because they are asked to advance their interests. Movements started with first a demand that was generally rejected. Then a challenge. Then a confrontation, and those confrontations lead to disruption.

KW: What keeps you doing organizing/movement work?

BA: As an organizer you make choices because this work is not easy. In this work you meet and work with phenomenal people. People who give their time, energy, and effort to advance struggles, to advance and correct conditions and improve conditions. They have accepted, supported, and embraced this work.

Another thing is witnessing and being a part of the changes that improve conditions. Working with phenomenal people and experiencing success together to get what people in the community want, whether a stop sign or ending state-sanctioned violence.

KW: What can you do if you want to get involved in organizing but don't know where to start?

BA: Understand that getting involved in organizing is a choice. It's not a nine-to-five kind of activity. You're committing to this work. If you want to maintain, and continue to do this, you've got to be willing to accept people where they are.

Secondly, be willing to understand and accept the victories, but also understand and accept the losses, and learn and grow from both. The contributions you make as an organizer are meaningful, valuable, and impactful. You don't have to do this for fifty years, for ten years, do it for as long as you can invest your time and energy to support others. Sometimes there isn't always

Kahlila rallies a crowd in downtown LA in November 2020 and warns them not to get complacent.

Organizing involves public speaking and marching, but for Kahlila it can also include moments of rest and joy with a puppy or a skateboard.

Nalleli has been in the spotlight from a young age. She was featured on a protest poster, has spoken to city councils, won the Goldman Environmental Prize, and was named to the Time100 Next list.

Sonia setting up for the arts justice event in Silverlake.

Amir Whitaker, her mentor, sets up along with the students.

For the Silverlake event, Sonia and the team put together an exhibit to "simulate a classroom as envisioned by student artists."

Sonia Patel Banker, 11th grader, San Francisco, CA:

Youth Liberty Squad

I was one of the students to initially draft the petition to **support counselors not cops and arts not arrests,** and eventually became one of the students to speak at meetings with state officials.

ACLU CALIFORNIA ACTION

aclu_calaction • Following

aclu_calaction ACLU's @YouthLibertySquad met with state education leaders to discuss how to ensure that California schools devote resources to school-based mental health in state budgets and governing.

California schools need thousands of additional counselors, nurses, social workers, and psychologists. Hear what Sonia has to say about why this issue matters.

Follow @YouthLibertySquad to stay updated with the youth-powered movement advocating for #CounselorsNotCops #ArtsNotArrests.

Liked by hitoshily and others
MARCH 10

Add a comment...

Much of Sonia's activism was on-screen, in meetings with state officials, or in the op-eds she wrote.

EdSource
HIGHLIGHTING STRATEGIES FOR STUDENT SUCCESS

TOPICS   AUDIO & VIDEO   PROJECTS   COMMENTARIES   DATA   PUBLICATIONS   ABOUT EDSOURCE

Donate   Subscribe

STUDENT VOICES

JUNE 27, 2021

SONIA PATEL BANKER

3 COMMENTS

For students in California, arts education is a civil rights issue

CREDIT: JOSEPH FANVU / PHOTO COURTESY YOUNG WOMEN'S CHORAL PROJECTS OF SAN FRANCISCO

Education Beat

EdSource

Subscribe on iTunes   Listen on Spotify

SPECIAL COVERAGE - UPDATED DAILY

How the coronavirus is reshaping education

or every student, whether attending school virtually or in person, access to an advice on how to be involved. If you want to do the work, then take the steps to do the work.

KW: How do you find your movement?

BA: Take the steps to find out what works for you. What are your interests? Is it ending police brutality, improving your community's health and eliminating food deserts, or closing the gender wage gap? Sometimes you might feel that everything interests you and you want to see everything change, but ask yourself, What are you going to dedicate your time and energy and commitment to? You can't do everything at once; give your time to one thing.

Another thing was identifying a person that guides you within the movement. If you're involved in a certain organization, identify a person in that organization, someone that guides you in the work. Recognize that another generation's success might not be your concern but has led to your work.

KW: How do you move past the valid concerns you may have about getting involved?

BA: Look at the success. Women getting the right to vote, ending Jim Crow, eight-hour workdays all have been substantive changes that organizers have to fight and put the effort to get. If these changes have been done, it can be done. It was because of people's movements.

KW: When do you feel that what you have envisioned and fought for will be accomplished?

BA: I want to live in a world where Black people can live their lives without being negatively impacted, without being negatively judged, without being negatively and despairingly taken advantage of. I want to live in a world that Black people have access to and capacity for improving the lives of the individuals, neighborhoods, their communities, and the environments they live in. This is why I have worked for so many years.

DISCUSSION QUESTIONS

1. Greg Akili, known to Kahlila and many others as Baba Akili, said: "Four conditions that I've observed that Black people face: white supremacy, institutional racism, individual bigotry, and mass denial." When have you observed or faced those conditions?

2. How did they make you feel, and how did you act on those feelings?

3. Amir notes that art can take many forms. What is an unconventional form of art you've seen or engaged with, and how can it be used for activism?

CHAPTER 9

SONIA

The early stages of activism aren't always particularly dangerous or glamorous or filled with action and protests and chanting. Sonia's first few months involved a lot of sitting in front of the computer.

She knew she cared about arts justice, sure, and wanted people to have access to art classes and the kind of creative outlet she had from choir—or could have at school, if she chose to partake in one of the many arts options her school offered. But to learn how to go about that, she had to learn what was missing and what had already been tried.

California law requires public schools to provide every student in grades one through twelve access to an arts education.[1] Amir asked Sonia to conduct a study of thirty school districts in California and comb through their education requirements to see if they include arts education. Schools offer classes based mostly on what their school district says they have to offer, and school districts are supposed to tell them they have to offer art.

Reviewing the curricula of thirty school districts was tricky. Even when Sonia found that a district required art classes in their curriculum, the high school didn't always offer credit for the class, and in some schools, there was only one class option that many students wouldn't be able to sign up for because of scheduling conflicts. This was especially problematic for students who wanted to attend a University of California school—the most prestigious of the public university systems in California—because the UC required a for-credit art course.[2] These are problems Sonia and her classmates didn't have to think about; they had ample access to every class needed to be eligible for pretty much any university. Unlike public schools, Sonia's school didn't have the restrictions of having to rely on the government, which sometimes demanded more than it provided the money for.

Sonia began to notice the gap between what school districts say they offer and what they actually offer. In the report, she wrote: "Reading through these results, most school districts list as having arts programs, but my surprise is that the amount of explanation around that subject is very vague. They write that arts instruction is key to the learning they do in primary levels, but judging from the lack of content written in Board Policy 6142.6 on this issue, it does not seem like this is valued."

Now she was ready for the next step, which was to convince people with power that they needed to give kids art access. She would use the data she had collected in the last month or so and also rely on her personal experiences with music.

"That really gave me the framework for, 'This is what I'm looking for. This is what's missing. This is what I have to do to address it,'" Sonia said.

By this point it was the summer of 2020. When the world shut down a few months earlier, Sonia lost the direct access to her friend group at the school lunch table, but at least the rest of them were athletes and got to practice together. As her sophomore year came to a close, Sonia began to see fewer notifications in the group chat with her friends.

Choir practice had gone online, but it wasn't the same as being in person, as feeling sound waves from your voice mix with everyone else's, then hit the walls and surfaces of the practice room and come back in beautiful harmony. Now the voices together in the same room weren't just a beautiful sound; they were a recipe for danger. Everyone became a box, on mute, in a Zoom room.

"There was only one sound wave and it's the sound wave you least want to hear, myself," Sonia said.

Some of that joy from music had transferred over to the work Sonia was doing with Amir—she enjoyed the weekly meetings and getting to know other young activists through the ACLU of Southern California's Youth Liberty Squad. She started a new group, the Arts Justice Council, and sought out middle and high school students through Amir's network and on social media. She formed a new arts journal, *The Road to Find*, and they put out their first issue as students returned to school. It was gorgeous, and Sonia was thrilled.

In the first edition, Sonia wrote: "Every child is forming an opinion about the world they live in right now, and those opinions matter so much. Students and children across the country are seizing initiative and are able to make some large and important changes, but in order to do so, they need to find their voice. *The Road to Find* is a journal that demonstrates that children have a voice, a story, and an imagination to make the world a better place."[3]

When she had those wins, Sonia felt the highs she missed from singing.

Still she felt sad a lot, and lonely a lot. And as Sonia would soon find out, activism also has lows.

PART 4

IN THE STREETS (AND BEHIND THE SCREENS)

I said, "Oh my God, the revolution is finally here!" And I just like, started screaming, "Freedom! We're free at last!" You know, it felt really good.

—SYLVIA RIVERA, transgender rights activist and Stonewall rioter[1]

CHAPTER 10

NALLELI

Nalleli peered into the crowd, and among posters with climate puns and calls to action, she also saw her own image.

Her face was illustrated on deep-blue posters, hair braided and over one shoulder, arms crossed, a yellow flower blooming behind her, and her image framed by the words "Youth Climate Strike."

Nalleli was marching beside Greta Thunberg, who had sailed from Europe to the United States to speak to the United Nations about human-made climate change and had spurred a local day of action in November 2019, when youth around the city were walking out of schools and marching the streets.[1]

As one of Los Angeles's most prominent environmental activists, Nalleli was part of the march, too—and a poster recycled from a global climate strike that September featured her as a California climate activist. Though Nalleli had been doing the work longer, Greta had gotten a lot of attention relatively quickly for the protest she began in Sweden, when she refused to attend school because her country wasn't doing enough to reduce their carbon emissions.

Nalleli and Greta met with other organizers and speakers before the march at a hotel near city hall, where many of the city's marches either start or end. Nalleli asked for a picture with Greta and immediately posted it on Snapchat to responses including "I love our president" and comments that the two looked alike with their braids and similar outfits. Greta and Nalleli jokingly called each other cousins, then shared their stories with each other as they began to march.

"Our community has always been pushed aside and ignored and neglected," Nalleli said. She was breaking that cycle.

By this point, AllenCo had stopped operations of the oil well and the city attorney had sued AllenCo in 2014 to keep it closed, resulting in a settlement in which the company promised to make certain changes and to pay more than $1 million to the city and county.[2] A coalition of local youth environmental groups, which Nalleli co-led, had even sued the city of Los Angeles in 2015 for putting their lives at risk by permitting oil drilling without adequate oversight. They settled the case in 2016 when the city implemented new regulations that required oil and gas companies to meet strict safety guidelines to get their permits.[3]

There was talk in the city of phasing out new oil wells completely, but it was going slowly. As of the 2019 climate march, LA's Energy, Climate Change, and Environmental Justice Committee had already postponed the item, which required discussion before it could make its way to the full city council for a vote.

The process had started in 2017.[4] It wouldn't get to the council until 2022.

Nalleli didn't stand outside Congress demanding change every day like Greta, but she did miss plenty of school to get these wins she was fighting for. She also missed a lot of the fun stuff that comes with school. Nalleli had to reject a promposal because she was speaking at a conference early the day of prom. When boys asked her out, she asked them what their availability was three weekends from now.

She also learned quickly that no matter how much change you effect, people will find something wrong with you. When she was honored in Miami at an awards ceremony, people online questioned how she could get on a plane and be an environmentalist. Other activists sometimes shamed her because she's not vegan.

"There's no perfect activist at the end of the day," Nalleli said. Because, of course, most people could always do more, herself included. She also knows, though, that the vast majority of carbon emissions come from a small subset of giant companies.[5] And there's a privilege baked into having the means to sail around the world or only eat vegan or never use a plastic cup, and there's even more privilege present in the demands that everyone else do the same.

"Sometimes you're only going to have access to a plastic water bottle," Nalleli said. "It's really sad and it hurts to know that something so beautiful like activism and politics can become so envious and power-driven and power-focused. You lose sight and the meaning of this beauty."

CHAPTER 11

KAHLILA

A protest can be so many things at once. It can be a forum to fight injustice, an artistic release, an outlet for anger, a birthday party. Watch Kahlila Williams protest, and you'll see all of the above.

After their first win—the slashing of LA Unified's police budget—Lindsay from GALA told Kahlila that she was going to join a protest demanding the ousting of the district attorney of Los Angeles, Jackie Lacey, a protest that had been going on every Wednesday for three years. Police had killed hundreds of people under Lacey's watch, and activists were angry that she had not tried to punish those officers, even though her job was to prosecute criminals, Lindsay explained.

When Kahlila heard about the protest, she was flying high after the school police victory she had helped achieve the day before. So, still full of fire, she went to the Jackie Lacey protest on July 1 to learn more about this cause. She saw activists she'd met the day before, including Melina Abdullah, whom she calls "Dr. Melina," and the actor Kendrick Sampson. Melina cofounded Black Lives Matter Los Angeles (BLMLA) and is a professor at California State University, Los Angeles; Kahlila had seen her speak before and admires her. Kendrick is well known for his role in *Insecure*—or in Kahlila's case, for his role in *How to Get Away with Murder*—and was a fixture at these protests, as well as a founder of BLD PWR, whose mission is "to reimagine and realize the liberated future our people deserve."[1]

Over the summer and fall of 2020, Kahlila saw Melina and Kendrick at the district attorney protests and grew close to them. She learned what Melina's favorite refreshments were from the vendors who came to donate their time and resources to the protesters, and brought her sweet tea and fruit snacks in exchange for a hug. Kahlila also became friends with Melina's two older children, both teenagers who had been marching for justice their whole lives. She became a member of Black Lives Matter Youth Vanguard and taught other students from her school about police brutality.

And without fail, Lindsay drove Kahlila to downtown LA every Wednesday afternoon. The teenager danced with her friends and hugged the families of police brutality victims. She learned their names and stories and comforted some when they cried. Afterward, Melina often swooped Kahlila up and took her home, where she, Kendrick, the kids, and one or two other organizers ordered in food and watched *Lovecraft Country*. For the third or fourth time in her life, Kahlila had found a new family.

She even got wrapped into the BLMLA "Williams" contingent, which included Students Deserve director Joseph Williams. The two are so alike in many ways, especially in their passion and ability to rouse a crowd, that Amir once affectionately called Kahlila a "mini Joseph."[2]

When Kahlila joined Students Deserve, she, like many of her peers, kept her camera off in her first Zoom meeting. But as activity ramped up to defund school police, and as Kahlila took on a greater role speaking at protests while also recruiting younger students at her school, Joseph began to see her shine.

"Everybody sees that she's an amazing speaker and can lead chants and has all this fire. But not so many people see the behind-the-scenes work and effort and real love," Joseph said. "I think you have to have love for folks to be an organizer . . . and she just has a deep love for folks. It's a blessing and joy to be around her and to be blessed to be in her little ray of love."[3]

As Kahlila took action against injustice alongside Joseph and the other Students Deserve and Black Lives Matter youth, she found in Joseph a mentor who understood what it was like to come from a family that many people wouldn't understand, with an identity that doesn't quite fit into boxes. Joseph's parents were strangers when they wed, their marriage arranged through the reverend of the Unification church—an organization that many would describe as a cult. Joseph has a Black father and a Jewish mother, and his first name, Wonman, is Korean—bestowed by someone from the church. Ask how many siblings he has, and his response is, "Depends how you count."

"She really is like a little sister in a lot of ways," Joseph said of Kahlila. And as with a sister a decade younger, many of their conversations—especially the ones that included Melina's daughter Amara—revolved around the teenagers roasting Joseph for his fashion choices or why he hadn't trimmed his beard.

The day before Kahlila's seventeenth birthday, in October, she stood on the back of a truck holding a bullhorn, leading more than a hundred people in chants of "Black lives, they matter here." The truck rolled through downtown LA, past courthouses, city hall, and police headquarters—so many buildings where adults make decisions that Kahlila disagrees with. On other days protesters would exclaim, "She's so cute!" and "She's so little!" when she darted past them, five feet tall and quick, but on this day her voice boomed loud and sure (people tell her she speaks "as if she were seven feet tall"). She called out the names of people who were killed by police in LA and demanded justice for them. Her energy electrified the people around her, older activists and fellow teenagers alike, and they chanted back.

When she takes the mic or bullhorn, her voice booms and people listen. Melina says Kahlila is a natural organizer; she knows when to lead a crowd and when to pause, listen to what they are saying, and follow their lead.[4] She knows when to lower the bullhorn and dance.

Melina's younger daughter, Amara, was the person who led the crowd in singing Stevie Wonder's version of "Happy Birthday," outside the Hall of Justice. As a police helicopter buzzed overhead, the families of people who'd been killed by police in Los Angeles joined in the singing. Kendrick hopped on the truck flatbed, talked about how great Kahlila was, and gave her a shirt that said "Black Baby Lives Matter" in purple, with a pacifier printed between the words. When he presented it in front of everyone, she bent over laughing at the inside joke—some of the teenagers in Black Lives Matter Youth Vanguard, the kid/teen arm of the organization, resent it when adults called them "babies" instead of "youth." Kendrick, like a big brother to many, loved making fun of them for it. Kahlila wore that shirt to the protest the next week.

This outpouring of love was a show of thanks for Kahlila's months of work for the cause, as well as a break in the heaviness of their task and a way to celebrate her involvement in the decade-old Black Lives Matter movement she threw herself into in the spring of 2020.

The adults who organize these weekly actions build joy and variety into the movement so that people can stay involved without burning out. Sometimes that means a birthday break; sometimes it means sitting on asphalt and making artwork in the middle of a protest. At one Wednesday protest in mid-October, a small group sat on blankets on the asphalt, surrounded by stacks of orange paper napkins. An organizer gave Kahlila a hug—by now it was a common greeting between her and the leaders—and asked if she wanted to help make flowers.

"Sure!" Kahlila said gamely and sat down to join the artist before she knew why. She watched the person in front of her fold one of these napkins into a flower. There were over six hundred more to go: one napkin for every person who died in police custody or because of police violence during DA Lacey's tenure, according to the Black Lives Matter count (the coroner's count of police killings was lower, but still in the hundreds).[5] The 2020 election was just weeks away, and the activists planned to create an art installation with the flowers in the park across the street from city hall.

Spring Street, cleared of traffic by sheriff's deputies who blocked more intersections than necessary for this small protest, smelled like incense. It was hot for any month, let alone October, and the protesters-turned-artists were making their napkin flowers under an aggressively blue sky without a single cloud to filter the sun.

Kahlila weathered the heat in shorts and a VOTE shirt from a Levi's get-out-the-vote ad she appeared in that year. Around her, adults chanted as she concentrated on the task before her. She folded the napkin like an accordion, then cinched it in the center with a string. She peered at the thing in her hand, which did not in the least resemble a flower, and glanced around at what the people around her were doing.

A few more teenagers had joined them by then, all following COVID health guidelines by wearing masks, but sitting less than a foot from each other, some knees and elbows even touching. They were supposed to be six feet apart, but the pull of friendship was strong.

Kahlila watched the others for a few moments, looking unsure of whether she was making her flower right.

"Jackie Lacey must go. Jackie Lacey will go," the crowd chanted.

Kahlila started to pull out each fold so her napkin looked less like a lumpy bowtie and more like a peony. She still didn't look happy with it. Meanwhile, on the flatbed a few dozen yards away, Jesse Romero's dad talked to the crowd about la raza. When Jesse was fourteen, LA police shot and killed him not far from where protesters currently were. Kahlila knew of his story—not just because she'd heard his parents speak at these protests but because she was creating an installation featuring the children who police had killed, as part of her Project Knucklehead fellowship.

Kahlila was still trying to fluff up her flower. She gave it a look, like, *Wow, I'm not great at this,* then hopped up, and ran to the free snack table. The volunteers knew her, and when they directed her to the snacks she likes—a bag of Funyuns and a bag of grapes the size of her head—she tossed a "See, this is why I love you!" their way.

Kahlila slid down her mask and started in on the chips, as she plopped comfortably back down next to a friend who was trying to add to the flower pile.

At the end of the protest, she was back on the stage with other members of Youth Vanguard to end the action like they did every week—by repeating the words of activist Assata Shakur:

> *It is our duty to fight for freedom.*
> *It is our duty to win.*
> *We must love and support one another.*
> *We have nothing to lose but our chains.*

CHAPTER 12

SONIA

No. No way. Nope. What. What?

Sonia looked at her screen in disbelief. Months of research and writing and drafting and editing this petition and now arts was just . . . out? No way.

She had been working with an ACLU of California lawyer to help draft a petition to redirect funding from police and law enforcement into counseling, art classes, and other programs that support student mental health. The petition was supposed to be called "Support Arts, Not Arrest, and Counselors, Not Cops!" The plan was to send the petition to state lawmakers after organizers gathered enough signatures. But first they had to decide on the demands.

Sonia had drafted the petition with statistics about arts and wellness. In front of her, she saw all that work, all those numbers, crossed out on her computer screen in Google Docs' dark green "suggested cut" color. The "arts" part of the title was even cut. Now it just read "Counselors Not Cops." Instead of asking lawmakers to prioritize school-based mental health and art programs, it now focused on just mental health. There were still demands for removing police from schools, but how to use that money was not there. Gone were the demands to "redesign public education curriculums so that students receive proper Visual and Performing Art Education," the charts that showed how California students were enrolled in fewer arts classes than in some other comparable states, and the fact that arts access is different and unequal depending on the kind of school you're at.

Here's a thing about Sonia: She works hardest when she knows something is going to go in her favor. She's good at singing, spending up to twelve hours a day practicing and performing on weekends to improve her skills. She's good at school; studying secures the grades. When a problem arises that she doesn't know how to fix, her pattern up until this point had been to let it go.

But this happened in late August as her junior year was about to begin. For Sonia's whole life, people had been telling her this was the most important year for her future. She had the pressure of classes and leadership roles in school and choir—including online meetings due to COVID, but these meetings didn't have the same payoff as meeting in person. Sonia had begun to feel deeply unhappy and anxious without her usual stress-relief outlets. She was stuck, mostly at home, caged in by public health restrictions outside and her own feelings inside. At most, she could draw or paint with watercolors and take daily walks to get out the restlessness and pain, often with the same song playing in her earbuds. The idea that sometime in the future, some other teenager might feel the way she felt—but not have access to art or other activities that provided emotional outlets—was unbearable.

So maybe for the first time in her life, she fought back.

In an email to the ACLU attorney who had edited her petition, Sonia introduced herself as the sixteen-year-old who had been working on this petition with Amir and wrote, "I noticed that the section on arts equality was completely omitted because it was not a priority for state-level advocacy. I was made aware that this petition was intended to address student mental health, and I wanted to ask you why art was taken out of this section." She went on to talk about her personal relationship to music, which was like a friend that kept her company when she felt alone, and pointed out that arts-based organizations already knew the petition was coming and could potentially get thousands more signatures if they were included. Counselors are of course vital, Sonia allowed—but often art is a way into self-care for people her age, a form of care that's vital to maintaining mental health. She also attached the first edition of *The Road to Find*, the arts journal she was about to publish. "Perhaps seeing how these students use art as a way to express solidarity and pain will help persuade you that art is so much more than just a second-tier social justice issue," Sonia wrote.

The email comes off as passionate but exceedingly polite, yet behind the formal words sat a seething Sonia. She had thought of the ACLU as a do-good organization that cares about all the issues. But that day Sonia learned a lesson many activists must face— the fight over who to include in advocacy often begins within an organization.

One phone call later, the arts statistics and demands went back into the petition, which then garnered more than five thousand signatures. In emails a year later, that same lawyer would use Sonia's arguments to appeal to advocacy partners to lobby for a bill that would increase access to arts programs for kids.

Sonia was becoming a face that arts people knew in California. Throughout the summer and fall of 2020, she spoke at online events to other teens and to advocates around the state about how art helped her mental health and how vital it was to students in California. Sonia's cup of chamomile tea resting atop a coaster that reads "Happiness does not depend on what you have or who you are, it solely relies on what you think" would grow cold as she'd talk passionately about how more money would help get arts resources to her peers. The 2020 election was coming up and in addition to deciding whether to oust the US president after one term, Californians would be voting on a measure that would give more funding to schools.

Once the petition appeared on the ACLU's website and started getting signatures, Sonia thought that would be it. She thought back to the petitions her classmates sometimes submitted to their teachers, demanding new snack options. Those just "kind of fell into this void" and nothing really changed, she said. She figured that after working with the ACLU for a year, just learning what a petition was and how to write one was valuable—she had started off writing down how she felt about art, and Amir had coached her on how to include statistics and demands.

It's not like anyone had to listen to or act on her demands. But as Sonia was learning, the path to meaningful and long-term change can sometimes be slow and repetitive. "It wasn't like the petition went to [California governor Gavin] Newsom directly and he was like, 'Sonia you're amazing!'" Sonia said. "But I think it contributed to a movement of saying—kids need these resources in schools."

The measure to give more funding to schools did not pass. But after the election, in 2021, elected state lawmakers and members of the California State Board of Education (there are a lot of different people who oversee education in this state) met with Sonia, Amir, and others from the ACLU and Youth Liberty Squad to learn about the petition, its demands, and the need for services that would improve students' mental health—like in-school access to counselors and art for those students who needed an outlet. Soon it was clear that the people who made decisions in the country's biggest state knew Sonia and her work.

"That was cool, because then I felt like in all aspects of state legislation, someone had some idea of what we were saying, and if the decision about government funding was being made, then someone might have had some understanding of what we said," Sonia said. It's really hard to know if there was a direct line from a petition to more money or arts programming for kids. "But you know that if someone mentioned arts, and someone who was at our presentation or got that email heard about that, that rings a bell for them. And that's a kind of cool thing."

RESOLVING CONFLICTS WITHIN MOVEMENT WORK

Kari Mallki is a healing justice organizer at Restore Oakland, where they use the framework and practices of restorative justice, and their training in social work and therapy, for conflict transformation work.

The premise of Kari's work rests in the understanding that while disagreements can get big and explosive fast, finding resolutions actually requires the slow work, over time, of creating feelings of safety within a group of people so they know they will be okay even if they bring up a hurt. That's vital to the work Kari does at Restore Oakland, where the group focuses on increasing residents' capacity to make their community safer before bad things happen, instead of relying on police after they do.

They shared advice on how to deal with conflicts when they come up in movement work—which is often.

SONALI KOHLI: What is restorative justice?
KARI MALLKI: We live in a society that's very carceral, that's punitive. That's based on retribution, and,

also other types of policing and surveillance and punishment, rather than on connection, care, understanding. And restorative justice is a way of thinking about what happened in our relationships and within ourselves back when harm occurs, or when we're feeling hurt, whether it's just something that we're feeling, by ourselves or in a relationship, what do we do to support ourselves in accessing care and in restoring our relationships with other people or with ourselves.

SK: If everybody is coming from the same place and they want the same thing, why does conflict happen in the middle?

KM: Generally, the way I think about conflict is that unmet need is present. So that can sometimes be super structural, like folks just not getting enough sleep, don't have a really safe place to be, they're less able to regulate their nervous systems and less able to just take a breath and not take things super personally.

Oftentimes, the unmet needs are much more emotional, right? Like feeling like your work isn't being valued or feeling like your voice isn't being heard. Feeling alone, or a lack of community, lack of acknowledgment.

And when we don't have the ability to be patient with each other, I think that's when conflict comes up, regardless of us having common goals. We think of conflict as something that we will hopefully grow stronger from, if we can handle it in a healthy way and if we can hold each other with grace through it.

SK: Tell me more about conflict being generative.

MK: I don't think the goal in our movement, regardless of us being on the same side, is that we all have the same opinions and perspectives. I really value learning from folks who are coming from really different places. I really appreciate being in circle and restorative justice spaces, hearing from folks that are even not aligned with me sometimes, because I notice that my body is in a space where I'm not activated. I'm really deeply listening and I can hear someone say something that would in another moment make me bristle and want to lash out. But I can hear it and think, Why did that person say that? What is bringing them to that conclusion about X, Y, or Z? Or why did they think that's okay, and actually try to understand that rather than just feeling angry about it. And I can feel angry about it. But that doesn't have to be the only thing that I feel.

SK: How do you deal with conflict within an alliance over political strategies or what to advocate for in the moment?

KM: By design, within the system we live in, we have to work with people who are not 100 percent on the same page as us about strategy. So it makes sense that we're going to disagree about some things.

We need to have points of unity. And those need to be determined probably in the beginning stages of our work together, so that we can know, yes, each of us has our own lived experience, our own professional experience, and our own long-term goals. But when we work together, this is what we need to be aligned about and focus on. And then, you know, there's still going to be disagreements that come up about how we allocate our time and resources, probably. There will be times when our goals even within those points of unity will contradict one another too much to feel good about how we're moving forward. But I think it has felt really necessary to be like, if we're going to work together, here's our non-negotiables. And here's the places where we can allow for more extensive conversation, and maybe compromise. If we care about this work, we need to be stronger than the systems that are going to continuously try to tear us apart.

SK: How do you decide points of unity?

KM: We work in a modified consensus model. So it's literally like, we just go around and around. If we decide something, and then people are dissenting, there's a very clear structure for how we move forward. And we can't move forward with a major decision unless we have X number of people who are down. The other thing is, if you're in this coalition and we decide—based on this model that we set forth in the beginning as a group—to move forward, and you disagreed, don't just leave. Because we've already assumed that we're in this together, sometimes we're not going to get everything we want. And that is just part of the struggle. And so I think it's recognizing that unfortunately, we cannot have it all. And we have to keep on fighting. And especially with political work, the wins are so few and far between, and the fight is so long.

SK: Youth have always been involved in movements. And they've introduced and pushed radical ideas that over the course of a generation become not radical at all. I think a lot of conflict can come from that. So if you're a young person and you have that fire, how do you engage in conflict resolution without becoming complacent?

KM: That visionary influence is the lifeblood of our movement. You need to have your people so you can feel like, here's the world that we're building together. Here's the world that we build in our co-op housing, or here's what we do on the side with art with the people who we deeply trust. And then we come together and think about some of the political work where it feels difficult to integrate that visionary framework fully. But to have the people that you care about and trust and are aligned with you, be there with you to hold each other through that.

SK: Let's say I'm seventeen. I'm in high school. What do I do to resolve the conflict? What does it look like?

KM: Conflict resolution and restorative justice practices are not a science. It's definitely something that's more of an art form that looks different for different groups based on your cultural backgrounds and your needs around what traumas you've experienced and what your access needs are.

There's this idea that like the prison industrial complex, we should have uniform ways to deal with things. With a restorative or transformative approach to conflict, it's wildly not uniform. It's extremely case by case, and it's extremely emergent.

And we're also relying on some tenets of nonviolent communication. If you can be able to breathe through things that are hard and speak in a way that's not inherently harmful and triggering for folks, and listen with intention, that's going to solve a lot of the problems. And even if you're not 100 percent aligned on things, you're able to treat each other with respect and probably have the awareness—you're not so activated that your amygdala stops you from being able to internalize new information. Part of how you resolve conflict is actually being able to change your schema and be, like, "Oh, that is interesting. I didn't know that before. Let me think about how that resonates with me or doesn't."

1. Have you ever had a conflict with someone who has the same ultimate goal as you do? How did you resolve it?

2. Would you have handled that conflict differently using these practices?

3. How can you incorporate restorative justice practices into your relationships?

CHAPTER 13

NALLELI

It seemed as if everyone around Nalleli was becoming an activist and marching the streets, demanding justice against police brutality in 2020. But Nalleli was in the unfamiliar role of observer rather than participant. She watched from home, recovering from surgery, then scrolling from the hospital, where she was undergoing chemo alone.

Her doctors questioned the occurrence of this rare and aggressive reproductive cancer in someone so young, but Nalleli thought often about the sign across the street from her childhood apartment, on the oil well, that warned of the chemicals that could cause cancer. By this time, Nalleli and her mother lived miles from that well. And it had been shut down. But Nalleli had never stopped needing medical care. Since her period started, she'd been in excruciating pain, suffering through symptoms including fatigue, brain fog, and cramps far more painful than any period should be. The medical system is rigged against Nalleli, though—research suggests that low-income women and children of color, especially Black and Latina children, receive substandard medical treatment and are dismissed without their serious problems getting addressed.[1]

At one visit to the hospital, a male doctor stood in the doorway of Nalleli's room and told her the emergency room was for "extreme cases" and asked why she was there. Other doctors told her she just needed birth control to regulate her hormones, even after she'd tried seven different kinds without changes to her symptoms.

"Cancer specifically taught me that I have to fight for myself and it's okay to put yourself first, and you have to in some situations," Nalleli said.

Finally, she saw a specialist at USC, who immediately told her this didn't seem like a hormonal issue and recommended doctors she trusted within Nalleli's healthcare network. One of those doctors examined Nalleli and found that she had polyps. These are small growths that usually aren't cancerous, the doctor told Nalleli, but they can cause pain. Still, they'd test the ones he collected just in case.

A week later, the doctor called and told Nalleli that she and her mom needed to come to his office first thing the next morning. She texted her best friend, afraid of the worst. Don't worry, her best friend responded, "It's just your anxiety."

It wasn't. As soon as the doctor started talking, his voice cracked from emotion and he had to clear his throat as he delivered the news: reproductive cancer, the kind that spreads fast. Nalleli thought of her three siblings, the loving household of eight she grew up in, the family she wanted for herself. She asked him, "Can I still have kids?"

The doctor's eyes began to water as he told her the treatment would most likely be a radical hysterectomy—a removal of Nalleli's reproductive organs, making it impossible for her to carry children. She soon chose to delay her surgery so she could freeze her eggs, and there were other paths to having children, but at nineteen Nalleli knew she could never become pregnant.

The surgery that followed removed six organs, and there still wasn't a guarantee she'd live. Doctors told her that her passions—getting a pre-law education from college that she had just enrolled in, Mexican folk dance, activism—they would all have to pause. She needed to stay alive first.

By now Nalleli was well known in activism circles, particularly in California and Los Angeles. She appeared on panels often, received awards, was constantly talking to public officials.

Nalleli was used to fighting for her community and for resources so that future generations of Angelenos would have access to housing that wouldn't kill them. That is the core work of an activist. But when her life was the only one on the line, that became harder. It's difficult to ask for help, not to feel selfish, especially when you're well known and count celebrities as your friends—people assume you have all the resources you need.

But none of the lawsuit settlements against AllenCo had resulted in Nalleli seeing money—AllenCo only owed the lawyers who worked with her organizations, and the city and county. Her family's primary source of income was still her mother's job at Esperanza Community Housing, which didn't pay enough for quality care. They had to start a GoFundMe to raise money for Nalleli's care.

Then there's life "after" cancer.

People think when you don't have cancer anymore, everything gets better. It does not. Well, maybe it does for some people. For Nalleli, it did not.

First of all, it's hard to say you're cancer free—first Nalleli was in remission, which meant the cancer was getting smaller, or almost gone. Then she had "no evidence of disease," which can feel so vague: *We don't think there's cancer, there's no proof there's cancer, but who really knows, you know?*

Also, recovering from surgery, radiation, and chemo hurts. A lot. Doctors had found and eradicated the tumors, but in doing so they had also taken out a half dozen organs and twenty lymph nodes. Lymph nodes, she learned, are body parts she never thought about but they did a lot, including draining fluid in your body. Without a big chunk of them, Nalleli could get inflamed and the buildup of fluid had nowhere to go. In time, doctors said, her body would adjust to its new resources and she should feel better. But it could take years.

For now, pain.

So much that Nalleli couldn't go back to school, even though it was virtual. So much that in order to do the interviews or appearances she committed to, because she still prioritized activism, she had to disassociate from her body to get through them. So much that she realized maybe she wouldn't be a lawyer. Meanwhile, the well across the street from her old apartment was still leaking. Los Angeles's city attorney filed criminal charges against the company's leaders in August 2020, saying they had not taken the right steps to close the well's operations and prevent leaks or explosions. AllenCo said it was the archdiocese's responsibility, but the archdiocese tossed the blame back to the oil company.[2]

Nalleli was sick, literally, of seeing these men ping-pong responsibility for a community, while she and so many others suffered for years.

Here's the thing about cancer, Nalleli said, "It makes you reevaluate your whole life."

Maybe every life decision from here out would have to take into account that she survived cancer, that she was still surviving it, that it could come back and she wanted to keep surviving. Maybe instead of law she should take on a job that required less school and less stress, that paid enough for her to cover medical bills that she was sure would continue to pile up, that would allow her to still be an activist but not rely on activism for her salary.

Nalleli started looking into diagnostic medical sonography—the job of someone who takes and analyzes ultrasounds. It followed what she had wanted to do before, in a way; when she was fighting for a safe community, she wanted to be one of the lawyers who fight for everyone. When she was under the care of medical professionals, she wanted to be a person who treated patients the way she wanted to be treated—with empathy, kindness, care, and respect.

When a Boston public radio host asked how she was doing, she said that at each of her quarterly checkups, she would think, "I just want a three-month pass. That's all I need."[3]

CHAPTER 14

KAHLILA

The lead up to the 2020 election was busy, but Kahlila loved the work. She loved marching and protesting, loved organizing on Zoom, loved teaching her peers about the different propositions on the ballot or the history of policing in the United States. She and the other members of BLMLA's Youth Vanguard walked from house to house in South Los Angeles, asking residents if they were planning to vote and explaining why, in addition to voting for president, they should look further down their ballots for a California proposition that would bring local schools more money and for a different district attorney who might actually prosecute cops who kill Black people.

Kahlila, who had just turned seventeen, watched as the Wednesday protests became marches to different polling stations where folks dropped their ballots. Every week Joseph and Melina celebrated the first-time voters. Kahlila wistfully watched as some of her eighteen-year-old friends put their ballots in drop boxes for the first time, or walked into downtown LA's regal Union Station to vote early. She wanted it to be her.

"It's sucks that I can't vote because this is a really big election year, and I really wish I could," Kahlila

said. "But at the same time, as much as I've been doing—trying to inform people about what propositions
to vote for, who to and not to vote for—I feel like in a
sense I am voting."

And she loved the victories. On November 7, the
Saturday after Election Day, Kahlila was already scheduled to emcee a rally, and to march with a group of
organizations, including local unions and BLMLA, to
"defend democracy" and demand a fair vote count. But
that morning, news organizations resoundingly projected Biden the winner of the 2020 presidential election. Earlier in the week, Jackie Lacey had conceded
the race for district attorney, and a local measure,
which would redirect a chunk of money in the city's
budget to alternatives to incarceration, also passed.

Kahlila felt powerful, her eyes piercing above a face
mask that bore a photo of Nipsey Hussle at a Lakers
game on one side, and the team's logo on the other.
To many LA residents, Nipsey Hussle was a man who
made it big in entertainment and reinvested money
and resources into his own community's success. That
community reinvestment and success are what Kahlila
wants. She's also a sports fan and forfeited watching
many Lakers and Dodgers playoff games to work toward liberation.

Atop the flatbed between Melina and Amara,
Kahlila danced to a playlist of carefully curated songs,
including "Higher" and "This Is America," all meant
to celebrate, inspire hope, and remind people that their
oppressors are still out there. Kahlila glanced over at
the Los Angeles police officers in riot gear lining 1st

Street, zip ties hanging from their waists in preparation for mass arrests, some holding shields, others holding weapons that shoot painful and sometimes fatal rubber bullets. Kahlila told the crowd not to pay them any mind, not to engage.

She leaned over the wooden rail of the truck's flatbed as it crawled slowly through downtown, trailed by a dense crowd of people chanting and dancing their way toward city hall. "We got Trump out of office," she screamed, her voice shredded from all the shouting she'd been doing lately. "And now we have to organize to keep Biden accountable!"

She wanted everyone to know: This wasn't just a celebration. This was the beginning of the fight.

CHAPTER 15

SONIA

By summer 2021, a lot had changed. Sonia had started going to school in person again, part time. She was about to start her senior year, about to join the softball team for fun. The pandemic wasn't over and so she still couldn't perform like she used to. But she did perform in a new way.

After convincing the ACLU to include arts justice in their petition, the organization sent the petition to the governor, the heads of the government education committees, the California Department of Education superintendent, and the State Board of Education—so many adults in one government system, so often disconnected, deciding who gets what money and how to spend it. Sonia went on a kind of virtual speaking tour with Amir as her co-presenter and cheerleader. She told all the adults about her love of music, about the journal she started. She and other students from the Arts Justice Council talked and talked and were told they was making a difference, but months passed and the laws and the rules and the money for the arts stayed the same.

You finish high school in four years, then you're an adult and you leave. So it can feel like you have to achieve massive systemic change in that time. For adults, time passes differently. Years run into other years and decades, and by the time anything changes there's a whole generation of kids who are adults and didn't have the things they needed growing up. So while Sonia appealed to the adults in the state to increase access to arts for children, she also was finding and making that community for herself and for the other students. Because they were all living through a pandemic and all its hardships, they needed an outlet now.

She met every two weeks with a group of students from around California who formed the ACLU's new Arts Justice Council. They shared experiences with art and their fights to get more of it in their schools; they planned actions and published *The Road to Find*—named after a line from a Langston Hughes poem—that came out every three months, featuring art submissions from students. Sonia led this effort, and the group became a lifeline. Sometimes the council of teens talked not just about the work but about what colleges to apply to. After the 2020 election, the students shared pictures of their siblings dancing and messages of relief. In their meeting after the election they held an unstructured art time. Sonia, once again, was making new friends.

Together, the council came up with different themes for *The Road to Find* journals, collecting art about the Black Lives Matter movement and police brutality, the 2020 election, environmental justice, and mental health care. Students won prize money if their fellow student judges selected their work as the best of the quarter. Plus, Amir printed at least fifty copies of each edition through Project Knucklehead, and eventually the ACLU would pay some of the artists to turn their art into thousands of stickers and postcards that have been mailed out to ACLU supporters.

The first edition of the journal was titled "Black Lives Matter, Black Arts Matter" and featured student drawings, poetry, collages, photos, calligraphy, and even music.[1] If students couldn't create or learn art in school like they should, they could become artivists with Sonia, but they could also make art with her, for her, for anyone who wanted to experience it.

And now, after months of meetings entirely on Zoom, Sonia had a chance to meet Amir and some of her new friends in person at a protest in Los Angeles that happened every Wednesday outside Amir's office— the ACLU of Southern California building across the street from the downtown Los Angeles police union headquarters. The police union negotiated on behalf of Los Angeles Police Department officers for things like salary, benefits, and protection if they did something like kill a Black person. That protection played a big role in keeping these officers on the streets. After the 2020 election in which activists like Kahlila and LA voters ousted the district attorney, Jackie Lacey, BLMLA moved its Wednesday protests to the union building.

The ACLU of Southern California very intentionally had a giant mural painted on the side of their building facing the police union, with massive images of Los

Angeles activists working to bring them down. Anyone going into the building across the street would see the faces of the communities they'd harmed.

That was the backdrop. At every one of these weekly protests, families could speak about the loved ones they'd lost to police brutality and ask for the change they wanted. Often there were moments of healing—breathing, yoga, libations, arts. And on this day in July, Amir, Sonia, and local Arts Justice Council members showed up with posters they made in favor of arts funding and bucket drums.

It was a hot day, sun beating concrete, and slightly smoky from burning incense. Sonia listened for the first time to families of those who police had killed as they spoke of their pain in English and Spanish. She listened to the mother of Daniel Hernandez, who a police officer killed in April 2020, talk about the pain of losing her child, as people around her supported her even though they may not all understand Spanish.[2]

"It was so beautiful, but it was also really, really sad and gut-wrenching," Sonia said.

A few hours in, Joseph—one of Kahlila's mentors and the Students Deserve director—stood atop a makeshift stage and spoke.

> We are working towards a world that doesn't look like the one we still live in. That doesn't continue to steal our loved ones. That doesn't allow state agents to murder and oppress and abuse us without any accountability, without any consequence. We're working to build a world that loves us, that

cares for us, that values us and our lives and our
brilliance and our love and our creativity and our
potential. And we see our amazing-ass youth do that
all the time, right.

Joseph introduced Amir, who introduced Sonia
and the work the young people were doing to increase
access to arts, especially for communities who had
experienced trauma.

Then Sonia climbed onto the stage with a fellow
student musician who played the guitar, and they sang
"Somewhere Over the Rainbow," in honor of the lives
police had taken. A plant stood in front of them—the
one that BLM leaders pour water on as they say libations at the beginning of each protest, invoking the
names of their ancestors, the movement's ancestors,
and the loved ones they've lost. Sonia's voice rang
through the street, and the crowd watched in silence as
the song poured out, the only other sounds the guitar
and a slight wind.

Sonia had known she was going to likely speak
or sing, but seeing these families also made her nervous—this was a Black Lives Matter protest, and Sonia
is South Asian, privileged, and has not lost anyone to
police brutality. But the encouragement and response
from the crowd supported the assurance Amir had
shared earlier, that this was a space where respectful
solidarity was welcome, and that music like Sonia's can
be healing.

Kahlila was there too, as she was every Wednesday.
Since she and Sonia both worked with Amir, they had

seen each other online. But this was the first time they had met outside of a Zoom room. Later, before she closed out the protest with Assata's chant, Kahlila told Sonia she had the voice of an angel.

It was the first time in more than a year that Sonia had sung in front of an audience. It was unlike anything she'd ever experienced, and so different from attending or watching these rallies online. Here she reveled in "watching people's reactions and feeling kind of the atmosphere—the heat, the incense, people eating pizza, the snack cart going around."

It felt exhilarating. It felt healing.

She was ready to take on more.

CHAPTER 16

KAHLILA

By late 2020, Kahlila was spending hours slouched in front of her computer and was not getting much sleep—often she was up until 2 a.m. and she couldn't tell you why. She tried to keep her eyes closed until a few minutes before her classes started at 9 a.m., but sometimes she didn't open them in time and missed part of homeroom. About one night a week, she didn't sleep at all. At the last district attorney protest before the election, as she marched to the men's central jail, she had to hold her lower back to help ease the pain.

All this worried the adults around her, some of whom had been doing this work for decades. Kahlila, though, was more preoccupied with other thoughts.

"There's a lot of pressure on Gen Z" from older generations, she said. "Like, Oh, you guys are our saviors, and like, you're gonna be the generation that sees change." She worried that everyone else may be depending too much on her and her peers. For her fellowship with Project Knucklehead, Amir's organization, she worked to honor the children who police have killed, an important but emotionally exhausting task. She was trying to help liberate her people and also submit a competitive application for her dream school, UCLA, on time.

Kahlila meant it when she told adults after the election the work was nowhere close to over. It's easy to celebrate a victory and think that fight is over; move on to a different one. But that isn't how long-term change happens, Kahlila was realizing. Yes, they had succeeded in cutting more than a third of the police budget. Officers would not be at every high school campus anymore. But it wasn't enough to get police out of schools—$25 million may not have been a very big part of the school district's budget, but it was a enough money to make a tangible difference in student lives. Especially in the lives of Black students in the district. Kahlila and Students Deserve now were advocating to spend that money specifically on resources to help Black students excel emotionally and academically. They suggested doing that by allotting the money to the schools with the highest percentages of Black students. Yet the district's proposals wouldn't even target Black students the way the school board promised they would. There was even talk of letting former school police officers come back onto campuses with different titles, instead of hiring restorative justice professionals.

So that was the latest issue Kahlila was advocating for.

Meanwhile, after the election there were rumors that President Joe Biden might appoint Eric Garcetti, LA's mayor at the time, to be a member of his cabinet in charge of Housing and Urban Development. That was unacceptable to many activists who felt that

Garcetti had done very little to help the most under-served people in Los Angeles. So Black Lives Matter protested outside of his stately mayor's mansion every morning for almost two weeks. On the thirteenth day, a Sunday, the Youth Vanguard—which Kahlila was involved in—organized a day for kids. The tone would be celebratory, like a block party but on the street in front of the mayor's house. There would be breakfast and brunch foods and music, and parents should bring their children, organizers said.

"There was these two new girls, and they were talking about joining Youth Vanguard and it was their second protest," Kahlila said. This was supposed to be a fun way in. People had brought their puppies and there was at least one baby.

But that day, when Kahlila showed up, there were more police than usual. And the police had more gear than usual, which they were starting to bring out.

"I just thought they were going to try to scare us again," Kahlila said. But her friend, Melina's oldest child, with more experience at protests that got violent, noticed the signs: police in two lines. Helmets un-clipped from belt buckles to cover their heads. Shields up. Batons out. They started recording.[1]

Then one officer pointed toward the group Kahlila was in, and the police charged. Videos showed protest-ers using what they had for the picnic—a cooking pan, a water bottle—to protect themselves from an officer swinging a baton.[2]

Kahlila screamed as another organizer pulled her to the ground and away from the circle police had made around organizers, creating chaos. She frantically looked around for her friend and caught up to them moving quickly down the block. Kahlila was shaking, crying. She took out her phone and went live on Instagram.

She took a deep breath, sucking in tears as she held the phone in her hand and pointed it up toward her, showing her face, the palm trees, and a clear blue sky. "They blocked us in and just started charging," Kahlila said as the sound of a helicopter buzzed by. Kahlila's voice doesn't break often. In this moment it did repeatedly. "They're charging again!" she said, watching what happened down the street and crying, as her friend said, "It's okay, it's okay."

"We were just literally eating donuts and the police cornered us on both sides of the street and then literally just started rushing everybody and they saw kids on the frontline," she said, eyes glossy. She turned the camera toward people walking down the street.

After that, for a while, it was even harder to sleep.

In an online conference the next month, Kahlila and another Students Deserve activist talked about the weight of the work. "Take that space that you might need and then you can always come back. . . . There is no level of how you should or shouldn't act when it comes to activism . . . definitely take that time, come back to the space," Kahlila told the mostly college students watching. "I'm still working on it myself."

CARING FOR YOURSELF AMID MOVEMENT WORK

As you've seen in all three journeys, activism can be an incredibly rewarding experience, but it can also challenge you physically and mentally. I talked to Roya Ijadi-Maghsoodi, a child and adult psychiatrist and health services researcher at UCLA, who works to understand and then address mental health disparities within communities.

Roya became an activist in college after the September 11, 2001, attacks on the World Trade Center in New York. The organization she was a part of, Time for Peace, held weekly vigils for years to advocate for nonviolence. I talked to her about mental health care, what it even means, how teenagers can get it, and how activism can inform your future.

SONALI KOHLI: So what is mental health?

ROYA IJADI-MAGHSOODI: Mental health is basically someone's emotional well-being, their spiritual well-being, and their physical well-being, the way people function in society, how they can contribute to society and relationships with other people.

SK: Why does it matter that we have spiritual or emotional well-being or that we function in relation to other people or in society? Like why can't we just be alone in our rooms?

RIM: Well, we can sometimes. But mental health is important because we do we live in a stressful world. People are constantly dealing with stressors. So mental health is really kind of this ability to cope with stress, to cope with life. People talk about having good mental health hygiene, so being able to have the capacity to deal with functioning in the world and taking care of oneself.

SK: What are the resources that young people have to care for their mental health? And when should you start thinking about it?

RIM: It's really thinking about it on a continuum. First, the basic things are making sure your basic needs are met: Are you eating enough food? Are you getting enough sleep? Are you living in a safe place? Are you housed? There's ways to address mental health by just working on getting enough sleep, being able to exercise, being able to be outside, being able to reach out to supportive people.

And then there's also needing to see mental health clinicians, people who can help support your mental health. So for kids and teens, I think one place to start is the school. A lot of schools are thinking about mental health more and have counselors, have social workers, have school-based health centers where kids can go and seek mental health resources. There's also a growing movement of peers, so youth kind of acting as peers for each other and really leading the way and talking about how important mental health is.

If you're seeing a pediatrician or you're seeing a primary care provider, you can ask for mental health resources there to be connected to clinicians. And then we also have hotlines. There's the Trevor Project hotline where youth can call anytime or text. To get connected to resources in Los Angeles we have warmlines for the Department of Mental Health. There's also lots of digital resources online too, websites like CalHOPE in California.

SK: The way that you described mental health, it seems like the things that cause inequity on a societal basis also would cause differences in mental health. If you're a teenager, a lot is out of your control, like if you're getting enough food or sleep or are housed. So how do you deal with that?

RIM: Focusing on the things that are in your control, so you know, still trying to get adequate rest, still trying to form supportive relationships, finding an adult in your life that can support you, finding the peers that you can reach out to. And then reaching out for mental health resources if you need it.

But, yeah, we don't want to place this on an individual. We also need to make the world healthier for teens. We need to kind of address these underlying issues. We can make things less stressful for teens. The adults can do that. The schools can do that.

There are growing efforts to increase access to mental health resources for kids. We're talking about activism too, so I think we also need to be thinking about that. Like, how do we keep increasing mental health resources that are super needed right now?

SK: Can you talk about the way that activism, organizing, and agency can play in how you feel as a young person and your mental health?

RIM: There's lots of evidence that self-efficacy—feeling like you're able to take care of something effectively—can help your mental health. Being in like-minded groups, being in social movements with people that are working towards greater goals together, can help your mental health. For people who have undergone stressful situations or trauma, making meaning out of situations or turning these situations into activism all can help with mental health. And it's really great that a lot of kids are doing this. And then on the other side, it's also thinking about when it can be too much, also being able to also still focus on your own self throughout all of this as well.

SK: How do you find that balance of helping the collective and feeling better because you're part of that collective, but then also caring for your own self?

RIM: This is hard. I don't think in society we are teaching that balance to people. Really being able to check in with how someone's feeling—Are you getting enough rest? Are you able to give? Are you healthy?—during your activism, during all these activities that you're doing and then taking steps to address it. And also thinking about things more long term. So if this is going to be a long-term effort, how to keep doing this while not making yourself burn out or be exhausted in the process.

SK: When you're experiencing something like that, whether it's burnout or where your body is on the line for your activism, how do you deal with that?

RIM: There's an urgency to activism because you're addressing life-or-death situations and you're taking on these really important issues that people are not addressing. I do understand the urgency, but I think being able to take a step back and thinking about the long term, so being able to rest in the moment, knowing that you can come back.

I do think we can learn a lot from self-care. It's a kind of a buzzword now, it's gotten a bad rap a little bit but self-care does have radical origins. It came out of the Black Panthers, the need to work on community health because of medical apartheid. Lots of activists throughout the years have had to turn to self-care. So yoga, meditation, rest, because they knew this was a long-term effort. So, I think, for teens to kind of reclaim that and think about that as well. Because adults often are not telling kids to rest or these teens are doing these things on their own time with all these demands placed on them. So being able to internally check in and rest and knowing that's okay.

SK: Can a teenager be negatively impacted by something that is happening somewhere else or that doesn't impact them directly, like seeing videos of police brutality?

RIM: Teens can definitely be impacted by events that they're not in proximity to, that they're watching. There's research actually out of 9/11 where people watching footage of what had happened develop PTSD [post-traumatic stress disorder] symptoms. And I think now we're just constantly bombarded by social media and images and videos.

I think especially if you're from that community, or you have a connection, it can definitely affect your mental health. That can also be really hard globally. So if you're in a place where your institution or school isn't realizing that something globally is impacting you, that can be even more hard, if you're feeling more isolated. So really kind of tuning into that and limiting what you're watching and what you're viewing and knowing it's okay that you're not feeling okay about these experiences and that it's really valid what you're going through and feeling.

You can call or text 988 to connect to a national Suicide and Crisis Lifeline any time of day or night. To reach the Trevor Project hotline, which Roya mentioned, call 1-866-488-7386 or text START to 678-678.

DISCUSSION QUESTIONS

1. How do you keep track of how you're feeling?
2. What are your tools for feeling better when you're feeling depleted?

PART 5

THE FIGHT CONTINUES

Fight for your lives before it's someone else's job.

—X GONZÁLEZ, Parkland survivor and gun-reform activist[1]

CHAPTER 17

NALLELI

On the day that the Los Angeles City Council was finally voting on whether to ban new oil wells in the city, a day Nalleli had been working toward for more than half her life, she wasn't in the room where they voted (because of COVID). But she also wasn't in the living room with her mom, watching rapt. Through a haze of pain, Nalleli drifted in and out of sleep in her room on January 26, 2022, as her mom called out votes to her, because her insides felt like they were attacking themselves.

Nalleli came back to herself a few hours later and the vote was done. No one could open new oil wells in the city. And the council ordered a study to figure out how to phase out the oil wells that were already there over the next twenty years[1]—by the time Nalleli's nieces and nephews would become adults.

This was huge. As of the most recent report in April 2021, there were 704 active oil and gas wells in Los Angeles and another 1,335 that were idle. That meant, like AllenCo's wells, they weren't in use but may not have been closed up properly.[2]

When the mayor's office invited Nalleli and her mom a week later to the signing, there was no way she was missing it. That was the big moment; when the mayor signs an ordinance that a city council votes on, it becomes law.

It was coldish for Los Angeles—in the sixties—but a gorgeous, cloudy day. Nalleli woke up knowing it would be one of those days. Her body hurt all over and started swelling from the waist down. It was hard to move her legs. Still, she put on jeans, her STAND LA T-shirt, and a black zip-up hoodie. "I honestly felt like shit, but I still went cuz it's like historic. How can I not go?" she said.

Nalleli and her mother arrived on Thursday afternoon at city hall, a gorgeous building in downtown LA. She took a deep breath and flipped her internal switch—the one that taps into her resilience and says—*I will get through whatever is next until I can get into bed again and cuddle with my dog, Albondiga, and no one will know.* The sleeves of Nalleli's black sweatshirt tugged past her palms. She curled her fingers around them anytime the pain got too bad.

She and her mother made their way to the mayor's conference room, stood before the wood paneling etched with a quote from Cicero: "Fidelity is the foundation of Justice."

Here, Mayor Eric Garcetti told the small masked group assembled that Martin Luther King Jr. and Cesar Chavez had made history in this room. Now they would.

Those were a lot of feelings for Nalleli to absorb. How dare he make her feel this much. Not to be outdone, Nalleli thanked the mayor.

"Thank you, on behalf of my community, as a frontline community member, as a cancer survivor, for listening to us, for listening to the science and for being a leader." Nalleli pointed to the nine-year-old girl near her. "I get to look at this little girl and know in ten years" she won't have to make a decision between her life and her reproductive system. "After you sign this document I get to say Los Angeles 'was' the largest urban oil field in the nation," she told him.

She was crying. His eyes began to glisten.

Yes! Nalleli thought, triumphantly, doing an internal fist pump.

Made the mayor cry? Check.

"Let's look at the votes," Garcetti said as he prepared to sign the document. "Yes, it's unanimous," he said.

"Yeah, it's hard to believe," a councilman standing next to Nalleli said to her. "I never thought this would happen."

She side-eyed him.

"Oh, well, I knew it would," she said. "So say 'cheese' because they're looking at us."

After Garcetti signed the ordinance and gave her the pen ("I'm going to frame it!"), Nalleli sat down, the waves of pain overwhelming her but unable to steal her joy in this moment. Still, she and her mom left early. Bed was calling—but not before they got celebratory In-N-Out burgers, "like true Californians."

This was the start of a pretty epic 2022 for both Nalleli personally and for the movement she'd been in for a decade now.

Later that month, Nalleli got a call from an unknown number while she was out getting boba. She answered, mouth still wrapped around the straw.

"Hello?"

"Is this Nalleli Cobo?" asked the person on the other line.

"Yeah, why?" Nalleli said around the boba in her mouth, assuming she was talking to a telemarketer.

The person was calling to tell her she'd been awarded the Goldman Environmental Prize. Still unbothered, Nalleli took another sip.

"Cool," she said, at this point used to awards. "What's that?"

Then she stopped chewing her boba, as she learned it's a prize awarded to a small group of environmental activists each year from around the world. Some call it the "Green Nobel." And it comes with a $200,000 reward for each recipient, to be used however they choose.

Nalleli thought she was being pranked, or it was a mistake. "When they told me, I was like, 'Are you sure?'"

For Nalleli and her mother, the possibilities felt endless, but this also felt like a lifeline. They had used up the GoFundMe money on treatment, and Nalleli still felt uncomfortable asking to be paid for speaking engagements. "This is real money that can set up not only me but my family for life," Nalleli said. They could invest it, but they could also make healthcare decisions based on what was best for Nalleli and her mom without worrying too much about the funding. That freedom is life-changing.

On August 31, Monic's birthday, Nalleli watched online as California lawmakers in Sacramento voted to outlaw new oil and gas drilling permits within 3,200 feet—about one kilometer—of homes, schools, healthcare facilities, and public buildings.[3] On Twitter the next day, she wrote: "Today is a great day for all californians we fought hard for years we persisted and we won. this is because of frontline communities that were invisible. si se pudo!!!!!"[4]

In October 2022, Nalleli was named one of *Time* magazine's 100 Next, which "recognizes 100 rising stars from across industries and around the world" for "their extraordinary efforts to shape our world"; she was nominated by her friend and actor Mark Ruffalo.[5] The day that was announced, Nalleli was once again experiencing painful cramps that made it hard for her to think straight.

But still, she celebrated. Still, always, she moved forward.

CHAPTER 18

KAHLILA

As she prepared to graduate, Kahlila saw a string of successes. Mayor Garcetti did not get to be part of the president's cabinet, a tangential victory but one to add to her list nonetheless. She continued to share her story repeatedly with school officials, in public meetings and private ones. And she encouraged younger students to do the same, bringing them in as leaders and sharing credit often. Kahlila was constantly trying to ensure that even though the students cycled out every four years, the movement remained alive.

One of the younger students Kahlila brought into the fold was Mani Sefas-Loos. Mani started ninth grade at the Girls Academic Leadership Academy in the fall of 2020 and, with Kahlila's encouragement, quickly became a part of Students Deserve. In September she spoke at her first school board meeting about further defunding school police—Kahlila and Lindsay gave her advice but supported Mani, saying whatever she felt the need to say was the right thing to share. Then, even though Mani had only been to a couple Students Deserve meetings, Kahlila asked if she'd like to present at the virtual Student Leadership Institute and teach her fellow Students Deserve members from across the district about the upcoming school board race. For someone who'd been looking for a way to become politically active, that kind of invitation in and confidence building can be integral to determining their involvement. She spoke at the February meeting and would continue to stay involved in Students Deserve once Kahlila was in college. By her senior year, Mani led the Students Deserve chapter at GALA.

"I feel like a lot of people who are in activism, and especially when they're younger, do it because they kind of want to make headlines and be famous and they want all the attention, but Kahlila . . . often gives leadership roles and opportunities to other people," Mani said.[1] "She obviously does want to have her own voice out there and she wants to say her piece, but she also cares deeply about the voices of other people and to put the spotlight on other people."

By January 2020, GALA girls made up a vital part of the Students Deserve team, and Kahlila was confident they'd continue to be involved in advocacy work after she graduated.

In Zoom rooms full of adults at the start of winter semester, Kahlila pushed back against the superintendent and negotiated with school board members, advocating for kids like her to get the resources they needed. Kahlila had a back-and-forth with the superintendent in one of these meetings, yet again explaining her experience and why cops on campus made her and many of her peers feel unsafe. January 2021 was a nail-biting month, and she wasn't sure what would happen with the school board vote in February.

There, she spoke publicly to the school board: "We organized, petitioned, conducted surveys and rallied to win this victory. It has now been seven going on eight months and yet this money still hasn't been invested back into Black students. We deserve to be able to get a high-quality education without being targeted or criminalized," Kahlila told the board, encouraging them to vote for a proposal that would allocate $25 million for "repairing the psychological, emotional, academic, and physical harm caused by the system of school policing."

"If you were listening, you would understand that school police caused harm to me and my community, and that is enough reason to abolish school police," Kahlila said. And beyond investing $25 million in Black students' education, she ended by reminding them of the long-term goal: "We must completely reimagine student safety by eliminating the rest of the $52.5 million LASPD [Los Angeles School Police Department] budget."

She spoke, the leaders she had trained at GALA spoke, Joseph spoke. The board members debated the details, consistently referring back to what students told them they needed.

Finally, the students won.

The school board adopted a strict plan that banned police use of pepper spray on kids, removed daily police officer presence from high schools, and made sure the $25 million funding would go to services like counseling and mental health care for schools with the highest percentages of Black students. In the Black Student Achievement Plan, district officials acknowledged the role that activists played in getting these resources now: "The perennial trend of black student underperformance paired with the current landscape of local and national advocacy for racial equity have served as the inspiration to act now."[2]

The months leading up to graduation were full of exciting, full-circle moments for Kahlila.

In March, she filmed an appearance on the Freeform show *Good Trouble*, a spin-off of *The Fosters*. Kahlila had watched both shows since she was little, and the actors in *Good Trouble* actually became involved in the movements they portrayed. Melina had played herself on the show in a storyline about activism, and Kahlila had met some of the actors at BLM actions. Another actor had become friends with Nalleli through environmental protests.

During filming, Kahlila was nervous, and she kept messing up the line, until the director told her to just explain what Students Deserve does as if she was talking to any group of kids. So she did: "We're a student-led, grassroots coalition that works to make sure Black lives truly do matter in our schools. Our overall goal is to get schools to stop criminalizing us and instead invest in us. We ended random searches, which was a racist policy that targeted Black and brown youth. And we're currently working on a campaign to get police out of our schools." That's the take that aired.[3]

The same month, Kahlila constantly scanned online forums predicting when UCLA decisions would come out. On the day they were released, she nervously opened the tab while on a three-person FaceTime with her boyfriend and her play brother. And then she screamed the happiest scream. She was going to her dream school.

But she wasn't going without making sure LA Unified heard her voice again. In early June, Kahlila left her graduation rehearsal early to trek to Beaudry, the nickname for LA Unified district headquarters.

"They were like, 'Where you going?'" Kahlila said to her co-organizers. "I'm going to an action," she had told her schoolmates.

One of the school board members, who was himself a principal decades ago, was advocating for police to be allowed on campuses at principals' discretion. Kahlila's action was to protest that resolution, which would not end up passing.

The large building blocked out the sun, and Kahlila danced in her dress and sandals to keep herself warm. Around 3:45, as organizers began blocking access to the street, Joseph and Kahlila got in a playful argument. The sun was out, he said, so why was she so cold?

"It's this stupid building!" Kahlila said. "They're blocking access to the sun!"

"Yeah, that's not the only natural resource they're blocking access to. I can think of a few more," Joseph retorted.

Then they got to work rallying everyone around them. Because, of course, the work was never done.

CHAPTER 19

SONIA

It was hard for Sonia to know what the impact of her work really was, especially with arts. *The Road to Find* had continued to publish, but the legislative process is slow, and the 2020 ballot proposition she'd been advocating for didn't pass. Was anyone reading these petitions? Were the lawmakers she talked to ad nauseum actually listening? Would they do anything?

"In a lot of art activism work, you can kind of question, 'Did I actually help anyone? Did I make large-scale change?'" she said.

But this, this was tangible. She had been overwhelmed when she first walked into the Silver Lake studio space that Tim Disney—yes, that Disney, whose grandfather was Walt Disney's brother and business partner and who was on the board of arts organizations—had offered up to the Arts Justice Council.[1] There was so much more room than she had anticipated filling, and the group had worked for two days, some of them nonstop, to bring it to fruition. Sonia had also started the weekend nervous—what if the rapport was different in person than online? But her new friends were just as friendly in person. In between setting up, they took little breaks to talk about school and their upcoming graduation and prom hairdos.

"It showed me that in two years we've been able to accomplish so much and do a lot. And this movement is not just a figment of my imagination anymore or something aspirational, but it's something I have done and created the foundation for people to continue."

Now the space was full. In front of Sonia, framed and on the wall of an exhibition space in Silver Lake, were the covers of all six issues of *The Road to Find,* surrounded by the artwork within those pages. And beside those pages, the first email Sonia had ever sent to Amir two years ago, almost to the day. Now if she spun in place she could see what her work for the last twenty-four months had yielded.

The student who had hung the covers would probably take over the Arts Justice Council soon, when Sonia graduated. Her movement had staying power. Across the hall was a canopy she'd erected that welcomed guests into the exhibition space, covered in student-made banners and sheltering two desks with student silhouettes, overflowing with flowers and art. It's a part of the exhibit Sonia put up and curated as the ideal classroom—full of art, color, and nature. The description that Sonia had written hurriedly fifteen minutes before read: "This exhibit simulates a classroom as envisioned by student artists, with color and art enveloping the classroom. In the imagination of the youth, the classroom is a place where they can grow, their voices can be heard, and their identities can be celebrated. Students have often referred to their schools as being 'creative dead-zones.' What if they were not?"

Throughout that Saturday, dozens of folks came through to check out the space, eat tacos and pan dulce, listen to Sonia and LAUSD board member Tanya Ortiz Franklin speak on a panel about arts justice, contribute to the collective mandala art, and get in on some bucket drumming that Amir led. They signed petitions, one encouraging the local school board to pass a resolution supporting more arts education and another asking the state leadership to allocate more funding to arts in schools—in addition to increasing after-school arts funding, which Governor Newsom had proposed in his budget. It turned out California would have a lot of extra money that year—as in, maybe around $49 billion extra—the richest Californians had continued to make money during the pandemic, and they'd pass along some of that wealth in taxes.[2] A lot of it would automatically go to school boards to serve students, because that's how education funding in California works. So there would be extra money for school districts to meet the requirements for arts in all the districts and schools.

Sonia flew home feeling excited and accomplished. A few weeks later, Amir forwarded her an email from his colleague—the same one that Sonia had fought with a year and a half earlier—calling on allies to support a bill in the state Assembly. The proposed law said that the youngest students received significant funding for arts education beyond class hours (after school, before school, lunchtime, etc.). This bill would make sure middle school and high school students got part of that money, too. It wasn't the funding Sonia had been fighting for—enough money for every kid to have arts education as part of their school day—but the words in the bill read eerily like that petition she had written some eighteen months earlier.

The Assembly education committee—the first group of lawmakers to read the bill, hear from supporters (and opponents), and discuss it—voted unanimously to pass it. Granted, there were multiple other groups of lawmakers who would have to approve it. But, still, Sonia was excited. *If it did pass*, she thought, *My words will go into law in the fall.*

That bill didn't end up becoming law. As fall approached, it got stuck in a file where California lawmakers put bills when they don't want to vote no but don't have money to vote yes.[3] Still, the resolution in Los Angeles had passed in June 2022, around the same time that California voted on its 2022–23 budget, which included the almost $1 billion extra for after-school arts education the governor had proposed, and $3.6 billion for schools to spend on "arts and music programs, obtaining standards-aligned professional development, acquiring instructional materials, developing diverse book collections, operational costs, and expenses related to the COVID-19 Pandemic."[4]

All this happened as Sonia was graduating from high school and preparing to move across the country for her next adventure—college and the art communities she'd become a part of there—knowing the *Road to Find*'s legacy was in good hands.

Sonia graduated and moved across the country for college. She made a new core friend group—one she could consistently connect with in person, finally. Back in California, there was yet another attempt to bypass lawmakers altogether and instead get California voters to approve of putting more money into arts education in public schools. It was largely funded, oddly enough, by local billionaire and former LA Unified superintendent Austin Beutner.[5] The facts and points of his 2022 campaign for Proposition 28 were many of the same arguments Sonia had made—in her research, in the op-ed she'd written for *EdSource*, and in the speeches to lawmakers.[6] Basically, if this proposition passed, the state would have to give schools money for arts education—on top of the money school districts already received.

Back in Philly, Sonia was singing again, the newest member of a campus acapella group. On Election Day, she voted for the very first time in her new city. Back home in California, millions of citizens voted also, and they passed the measure to fund arts education.

Activism doesn't have to be grand. It doesn't have to be big. It can be the small wins that turn into big ones, from one email, to one journal entry, to one change.

1. Why did the author put Kahlila's, Nalleli's, and Sonia's narratives together? What are the similarities and differences in their stories?

2. All three teen activists acted independently but had the guidance of adults around them. What were the elements or shared experiences that made for strong mentor-mentee relationships?

3. The author calls this a work of nontraditional journalism. How does this differ from other kinds of journalism you've read, listened to, or watched? Why do you think she took this approach?

ACKNOWLEDGMENTS

Thank you first and most to Kahlila, Nalleli, and Sonia.

Kahlila, this all started with you. Thank you for letting me follow you around for years (even when I was boring).

Nalleli, it has been a privilege to heal beside you.

Sonia, you're the teenager I wish I had been. I feel lucky to witness your journey into adulthood.

Shelly and Sunil Kohli, aka Mom and Dad, thank you for telling me always and often to do what I love. I am happy because of you. Also thanks for catching typos in my manuscript. Sneha Didi, sister code. Neil, thank you for becoming my brother. To Rohan, you bring so much joy to so many lives. I love you, and I hope you read this when you're older and know your joy is just as important.

Thank you to the many organizers, activists, researchers, educators, and kids who talked to me for this book and for my stories in the past, and who introduced me and vouched for me to others in the movements. There are so many people of every generation who have been doing this work, who continue to, who are not named in this book. Thanks to Tyrone Howard and Amir Whitaker, especially, for the many years of conversations and introductions.

Thank you to the Spencer Education Fellowship for the time, funding, and access to Columbia University classes and resources to start this book. LynNell Hancock, thank you for your kindness and patience. Lalitha Vasudevan, thank you for teaching me to broaden my reporting styles. Dale Maharidge, thanks for teaching me how to get a book published. Benjamin Herold, thanks for your openness and introductions. I feel like I wrote this book in so many oases. Thanks to the Soaring Gardens Artists Retreat and the Ora Lerman Charitable Trust, the Ucross Foundation, and Kylie Reynolds and the Spriggs Family for providing spaces surrounded by nature and peace for me to write and edit.

Tanya McKinnon is the greatest agent ever; thank you for telling me I can write one book and also then another one. Ian Lendler, thanks for your notes and your honesty and validation. Joanna Green, Alison Rodriguez, Susan Lumenello, and the entire Beacon team, thank you for treating these words with such care.

You'll see that I cite so so so many news articles in this book, especially from my former colleagues at the *Los Angeles Times*. Their work is vital so please support local journalism. Thank you to all the journalists who wrote those stories and so many more. Thanks especially to S. Mitra Kalita, who made me an education reporter, brought me back to LA, and has transformed what my dreams can be so many times with the possibilities she offers. The entire team at URL Media, especially Leonor Ayala Polley, made room for me to work with them and also to write and report this, and their generosity and kindness create the environment every workplace should strive for.

A lot of young people weighed in at every point of reporting and writing. Thanks to the ACLU of Southern California Youth Liberty Squad for telling me what you want to see in a book like this, and to the students who joined Beacon's teen advisory council for telling me so honestly what you thought about it and how to make it better.

A bunch of very vital but miscellaneous thanks: Gabriella Angotti-Jones for the stunning photos, Melvin Backman for your meticulous fact-checking. Joy Resmovits for your constant expertise and Emily Alpert Reyes for your generosity with sources. The 2024Ever debut authors Slack, a constant source of comfort that I was not the only one lost in the process. Dr. Adaobi Anyeji for being my therapist and making me understand feelings. Christina Hammonds Reed for your constant guidance and confidence injections, and Sophia Dalton for introducing us and letting me box out said feelings. Sim Sekhon for unconditional empathy. Franny Barnes and Karen Cheng for fifteen years of consistent chaos and patience. Sam Masunaga for letting me follow you to every milestone, and Yanting Li and Josh Cain for your friendships when I reached those milestones.

And thanks to you, for reading.

NOTES

PART 1: THE CATALYST

1. Bennito L. Kelty, "Activist Angela Davis Urges Cooperation Against Injustice," *Columbia Missourian*, January 24, 2017, https://www.columbiamissourian.com/news/local/activist-angela-davis-urges-cooperation-against-injustice/article_f77a21a0-e2b0-11e6-9d29-130699fe9e6d.amp.html.

CHAPTER 1: NALLELI

1. Zoie Matthew, "4 Oil Wells Hidden in Plain Sight in L.A." *Los Angeles Magazine*, February 5, 2018, https://www.lamag.com/citythinkblog/hidden-oil-wells.

2. Los Angeles City Controller, *Review of Oil and Gas Drilling Sites in the City of Los Angeles*, June 27, 2017, https://controller.lacity.gov/audits/review-of-the-city-of-los-angeles-oil-and-gas-drilling.

3. Louis Sahagún, "Crackdown on Archdiocese-Owned Oil Field Near USC Gets OK, City Attorney Says," *Los Angeles Times*, June 8, 2016, https://www.latimes.com/local/california/la-me-ln-oil-injunction-20160608-snap-story.html.

CHAPTER 2: KAHLILA

1. Sonali Kohli, "L.A. Unified Renames First All-Girls School After Retired Supt. Michelle King," *Los Angeles Times*, March 13, 2018, https://www.latimes.com/local/education/la-me-edu-michelle-king-school-renaming-20180313-story.html.

2. Lindsay Herz, interview by Sonali Kohli, November 16, 2020.

3. Herz, interview.

4. Terry Allen, Isaac Bryan, Andrew Guerrero, Alvin Teng, Kelly Lytle-Hernandez, and the Million Dollar Hoods Team, *Policing Our Students: An Analysis of L.A. School Police Department Data (2014–2017)*, Million Dollar Hoods Project, 2018, https://million dollarhoods.org/wp-content/uploads/2018/10/Policing-Our-Students -MDH-Report-Final.pdf.

5. Kelly Puente, "Protesters Decry School Cuts," *Long Beach Press-Telegram*, May 25, 2011, provided by Long Beach Public Library Microfilm.

6. Christian Wimberly, "Why We Need School Police by Dashaxn," Project Knucklehead, July 25, 2020, https://www.youtube.com/watch?v=HCQNM1eRk3M.

CHAPTER 3: SONIA

1. Kliptown Youth Program, "From Poverty to Opportunity," https://www.kliptownyouthprogram.org.za, accessed July 27, 2023.

PART 2: KNOW YOUR STORY

1. Malala Yousafzai, "Malala Yousafzai: 16th Birthday Speech at United Nations," Malala Fund, July 12, 2013, https://malala.org /newsroom/malala-un-speech.

CHAPTER 4: NALLELI

1. Hayley Smith, "California Still Highly Segregated by Race Despite Growing Diversity, Research Shows," *Los Angeles Times*, June 28, 2021, https://www.latimes.com/california/story/2021-06 -28/l-a-segregation-problems-unchanged-in-decades-study-shows.

2. Sarah Kuta, "Redlined Neighborhoods Have Higher Levels of Air Pollution, Study Suggests," *Smithsonian Magazine*, March 17, 2022, https://www.smithsonianmag.com/smart-news/redlined -neighborhoods-have-higher-levels-of-air-pollution-study-suggests -180979750.

3. Louis Sahagún, "Crackdown on Archdiocese-Owned Oil Field Near USC Gets OK, City Attorney Says," *Los Angeles Times*, June 9, 2016, https://www.latimes.com/local/california/la-me-ln-oil -injunction-20160608-snap-story.html.

4. Louis Sahagún, "Controversial Urban Oil Field Voluntarily Agrees to Halt Operations," *Los Angeles Times*, November 22, 2013, https://www.latimes.com/local/la-xpm-2013-nov-22-la-me -1123-oil-field-fumes-20131123-story.html.

5. D. J. Martucci, "Methods of Using Strong Acids Modified with Acid Solutions," US Patent, No. 4,675,120, June 23, 1987, https://patentimages.storage.googleapis.com/29/0b/3e/e0edd48 a1717d6/US4675120.pdf.

6. "Mapping L.A.: Wilmington," *Los Angeles Times*, https:// maps.latimes.com/neighborhoods/neighborhood/wilmington/index .html, accessed July 27, 2023; Tony Briscoe, "State Officials Draw Fire After Approving New Oil Wells in L.A. Neighborhood," *Los Angeles Times*, June 3, 2022, https://www.latimes.com/environment /story/2022-06-03/residents-fight-oil-drilling-in-los-angeles -neighborhood; "The Health Toll of L.A.'s Oil Rigs," *Living on Earth*, July 29, 2022, https://www.loe.org/shows/segments.html ?programID=22-P13-00030&segmentID=4.

7. Ingrid Lobet, "Troubled South L.A. Oil Well Site Remains a Danger to Locals," *Capital & Main*, co-published with *L.A. Taco*, May 26, 2021, https://www.lataco.com/south-la-oil-site-danger.

8. Louis Sahagún, "EPA Officers Sickened by Fumes at South L.A. Oil Field," *Los Angeles Times*, November 8, 2013, https:// www.latimes.com/local/la-me-1109-fumes-20131109-story.html.

CHAPTER 6: SONIA
1. Amir Whitaker, *The Knuckleheads's Guide to Escaping the Trap* (Los Angeles: KnuckleHead Publishing, 2016), 36.

2. Whitaker, *The Knuckleheads's Guide to Escaping the Trap*, 92.

3. Whitaker, *The Knuckleheads's Guide to Escaping the Trap*, 487.

4. Sonali Kohli, "Do L.A. Unified's Daily Random Searches Keep Students Safe, or Do They Go Too Far?" *Los Angeles Times*, December 26, 2017, https://www.latimes.com/local/education/la-me -edu-random-searches-school-20171226-htmlstory.html.

PART 3: FOOTPRINTS ON THE MOON
1. John Lewis, 2014 Emory Law School Commencement.

CHAPTER 7: NALLELI
1. "The Health Toll of L.A.'s Oil Rigs," *Living on Earth*, July 29, 2022, https://www.loe.org/shows/segments.html?programID=22 -P13-00030&segmentID=4.

2. Louis Sahagún, "South Los Angeles Residents Fuming over Oil Field," *Los Angeles Times*, October 16, 2013, https://www

.latimes.com/local/la-xpm-2013-oct-16-la-me-fumes-20131017
-story.html.

3. Louis Sahagún, "Controversial Urban Oil Field Voluntarily
Agrees to Halt Operations," *Los Angeles Times*, November 22,
2013, https://www.latimes.com/local/la-xpm-2013-nov-22-la-me
-1123-oil-field-fumes-20131123-story.html.

CHAPTER 8: KAHLILA

1. LAUSD Board of Education meeting, June 30, 2020, https://
lausd.granicus.com/MediaPlayer.php?clip_id=3650.

2. LAUSD Board of Education meeting.

3. Sonali Kohli and Howard Blume, "L.A. Schools Have Given
Up the Last of Their Defense Department-Issued Rifles," *Los Angeles Times*, February 23, 2016, https://www.latimes.com/local
/education/lausd/la-me-edu-school-weapons-returned-20160223
-story.html.

4. Sonali Kohli, "L.A. Unified Board Votes to End Random
Searches," *Los Angeles Times*, June 18, 2019, https://www.latimes
.com/local/education/la-me-edu-random-searches-lausd-20190618
-story.html.

5. Sonali Kohli, "Do L.A. Unified's Daily Random Searches
Keep Students Safe, or Do They Go Too Far?" *Los Angeles Times*,
December 26, 2017, https://www.latimes.com/local/education/la-me
-edu-random-searches-school-20171226-htmlstory.html.

6. Amir Whitaker, interview by Sonali Kohli, October 26, 2020.

7. Howard Blume and Sonali Kohli, "L.A. Unified Police Chief
Resigns After District Slashes Department Budget," *Los Angeles
Times*, June 30, 2020, https://www.latimes.com/california/story
/2020-06-30/lausd-unified-budget-school-police-reopening.

CHAPTER 9: SONIA

1. California Education Code, Title 2, Part 28, Chapter 2, Articles 2 and 3, https://leginfo.legislature.ca.gov/faces/codes_display
Section.xhtml?sectionNum=51212.&nodeTreePath=2.3.4.3.2
&lawCode=EDC.

2. University of California Admissions, "Subject Requirements,"
https://admission.universityofcalifornia.edu/admission-requirements
/freshman-requirements/subject-requirement-a-g.html, accessed July
27, 2023.

3. Sonia Banker, "Foreword," *The Road to Find*, August/
September 2020, https://www.theroadtofind.org/editions.

PART 4: IN THE STREETS (AND BEHIND THE SCREENS)

1. Sylvia Rivera, "Sylvia Rivera & NYPD Reflect on Stonewall Rebellion," 1989 Sound Portraits via *The Spirit Was . . .* , Tumblr, https://thespiritwas.tumblr.com/post/18108920192/sylvia-rivera -nypd-reflect-on-stonewall.

CHAPTER 10: NALLELI

1. Tony Barboza, "Greta Thunberg Joins L.A. Climate Strike, Says Wildfires 'Will Continue to Get Worse,'" *Los Angeles Times*, November 1, 2019, https://www.latimes.com/california/story /2019-11-01/greta-thunberg-youth-climate-strike-planned-for -friday.

2. Emily Guerin, "AllenCo Oil Company to Pay $1.25 Million to LA in Lawsuit Settlement," *LAist/KPCC*, June 9, 2016, https:// www.kpcc.org/2016-06-09/allenco-oil-company-to-pay-1-25 -million-to-la-in-l.

3. Ashley Braun, "After Los Angeles Youth Sued City for Discriminatory Drilling Practices, the Oil Industry Sued Back," *DeSmog*, April 3, 2017, https://www.desmogblog.com/2017/04/03 /youth-color-lawsuit-los-angeles-drilling-discrimination-oil-industry.

4. Los Angeles City Clerk, Council File: 17-0447, "Land Use Codes/Oil and Gas Development/Impact on Resident Health and Safety/Code Change Proposals," https://cityclerk.lacity.org/lacity clerkconnect/index.cfm?fa=ccfi.viewrecord&cfnumber=17-0447.

5. Tess Riley, "Just 100 Companies Responsible for 71% of Global Emissions, Study Says," *The Guardian*, July 10, 2017, https://www.theguardian.com/sustainable-business/2017/jul/10/100 -fossil-fuel-companies-investors-responsible-71-global-emissions -cdp-study-climate-change.

CHAPTER 11: KAHLILA

1. BLD PWR, https://www.bldpwr.com/about/, accessed August 14, 2023.

2. Amir Whitaker, interview by Sonali Kohli, October 26, 2020.

3. Wonman Joseph Williams, interview by Sonali Kohli, September 19, 2020.

4. Melina Abdullah, interview by Sonali Kohli, November 10, 2020.

5. Black Lives Matter, "Jackie Lacey Must Go," https://www .blmla.org/jackie-lacey-must-go, accessed July 27, 2023; *Los Angeles Times* Staff, "Police Have Killed 1002 People in L.A. County

Since 2000," *Los Angeles Times*, April 11, 2023, https://www
.latimes.com/projects/los-angeles-police-killings-database.

CHAPTER 13: NALLELI

1. S. Hamed, H. Bradby, B. M. Ahlberg et al., "Racism in Healthcare: A Scoping Review," *BMC Public Health* 22, no. 988 (2022), https://doi.org/10.1186/s12889-022-13122-y; J. R. Marin et al., "Racial and Ethnic Differences in Emergency Department Diagnostic Imaging at US Children's Hospitals, 2016–2019," *JAMA Network Open* 4, no. 1 (January 4, 2021): e2033710, doi: 10.1001/jamanetworkopen.2020.33710.

2. Emily Alpert Reyes, "Oil Company Allenco and Its Leaders Face Criminal Charges over Deteriorating Wells," *Los Angeles Times*, August 4, 2020, https://www.latimes.com/california/story/2020-08-04/allenco-lawsuit.

3. Nalleli Cobo, "'We Feed People' Documentary; Anti-Drilling Activist Nalleli Cobo Wins Goldman Prize," NPR, May 26, 2022, https://www.npr.org/2022/05/26/1101562727/we-feed-people-documentary-anti-drilling-activist-nalleli-cobo-wins-goldman-priz.

CHAPTER 15: SONIA

1. *The Road to Find*, August/September 2020, https://www.theroadtofind.org/editions.

2. Kevin Rector and Richard Winton, "L.A. Police Commission Rules Officer Broke Policy with Final Two Shots in Hernandez Killing," *Los Angeles Times*, December 15, 2020, https://www.latimes.com/california/story/2020-12-15/commission-votes-on-mcbride-shooting.

CHAPTER 16: KAHLILA

1. Thandiwe Abdullah, Instagram post, December 6, 2020, https://www.instagram.com/tv/CIdys3sJVVK/?igshid=ZDhmZGIxNmQ=.

2. Jaclyn Cosgrove, Kevin Rector, and Dakota Smith, "Los Angeles Police Converge on Peaceful Black Lives Matter Protest at Mayor's House," *Los Angeles Times*, December 6, 2020, https://www.latimes.com/california/story/2020-12-06/los-angeles-police-converge-on-peaceful-black-lives-matter-protest.

PART 5: THE FIGHT CONTINUES

1. "Emma González: 'Fight for Your Lives Before It's Someone Else's Job,'" CBS News, March 24, 2018, https://www.cbsnews

.com/video/emma-gonzalez-fight-for-your-lives-before-its-someone-elses-job.

CHAPTER 17: NALLELI

1. Dakota Smith, "Los Angeles Moves to End Oil Drilling in the City," *Los Angeles Times*, January 26, 2022, https://www.latimes.com/california/story/2022-01-26/l-a-city-council-moves-to-phase-out-oil-and-gas-drilling.

2. Office of the Los Angeles City Administrative Officer, *Report on Petroleum Oil Extraction Tax and Revenue*, May 20, 2022, CAO file no. 0220-05875-0000.

3. California SB-1137 Oil and Gas: Operations: Location Restrictions: Notice of Intention: Health Protection Zone: Sensitive Receptors. (2021–2022), September 16, 2022, https://leginfo.legislature.ca.gov/faces/billTextClient.xhtml?bill_id=202120220SB1137.

4. Nalleli Cobo, Twitter, August 31, 2022, https://twitter.com/NalleliCobo/status/1565199643016941569?s=20&t=tahE7mRGLGQtkC4fDGn5BA.

5. Time staff, "How We Chose the 2022 TIME100 Next," September 28, 2022, https://time.com/6216698/how-we-chose-time100-next-2022/; Mark Ruffalo, "Nalleli Cobo," September 28, 2022, https://time.com/collection/time100-next-2022/6213816/nalleli-cobo.

CHAPTER 18: KAHLILA

1. Mani Sefas-Loos, interview by Sonali Kohli, October 26, 2020.

2. Los Angeles Unified School District, *Black Student Achievement Plan*, https://achieve.lausd.net/cms/lib/CA01000043/Centricity/Domain/1334/Black_Student_Achievement_Plan_Final.pdf, accessed July 27, 2023.

3. "Making a Metamour," *Good Trouble*, season 3, episode 13.

CHAPTER 19: SONIA

1. Jesse Goddard, "Tim Disney's Kitchen Reflects His Colorful Family Tree," *Los Angeles Times*, April 26, 2019, https://www.latimes.com/business/realestate/hot-property/la-fi-hp-tim-disney-kitchen-40190427-story.html.

2. Alexei Koseff, "California Budget: Big Surplus, Big Differences," *CalMatters*, June 13, 2022, https://calmatters.org/politics/2022/06/california-budget-surplus-differences.

3. "AB-2507: The Universal Afterschool and Expanded Learning Opportunities Program: The After School Education and Safety Program: The 21st Century Community Learning Centers Program (2021–2022)," California Legislative Information, https://leginfo.legislature.ca.gov/faces/billHistoryClient.xhtml?bill_id=202120220AB2507, accessed August 23, 2023.

4. Office of Tanya Ortiz Franklin, Los Angeles Unified School District Board District 7 Board Member, "Arts Justice: Access and Equity Across the Disciplines and the District," https://drive.google.com/file/d/1qDpUMtQnQjl-PjNxwb0fMoa89XO25VIf/view, accessed August 23, 2023; *K–12 Education*, California State Budget 2022–23, https://ebudget.ca.gov/2022-23/pdf/BudgetSummary/K-12 Education.pdf, accessed August 23, 2023.

5. CalMatters 2022 Voter Guide, "Prop 28: Guarantee Funding for Arts and Music Education," *CalMatters*, https://calmatters.org/california-voter-guide-2022/propositions/prop-28-arts-education, accessed July 27, 2023.

6. Sonia Patel Banker, "For Students in California, Arts Education Is a Civil Rights Issue," June 27, 2021, *EdSource*, https://edsource.org/2021/for-students-in-california-arts-education-is-a-civil-rights-issue/656913.

IMAGE CREDITS FOR INSERT

1. Sonali Kohli
2. Gabriella Angotti-Jones
3. Gabriella Angotti-Jones
4. Gabriella Angotti-Jones
5. Gabriella Angotti-Jones
6. Gabriella Angotti-Jones
7. Tamara Leigh Photography/Goldman Environmental Prize
8. Courtesy of Nalleli Cobo
9. Tamara Leigh Photography/Goldman Environmental Prize
10. Courtesy of Nalleli Cobo
11. Courtesy of Nalleli Cobo
12. Gabriella Angotti-Jones
13. Gabriella Angotti-Jones
14. Gabriella Angotti-Jones
15. Gabriella Angotti-Jones
16. Gabriella Angotti-Jones
17. ACLU California Action
18. Courtesy of EdSource